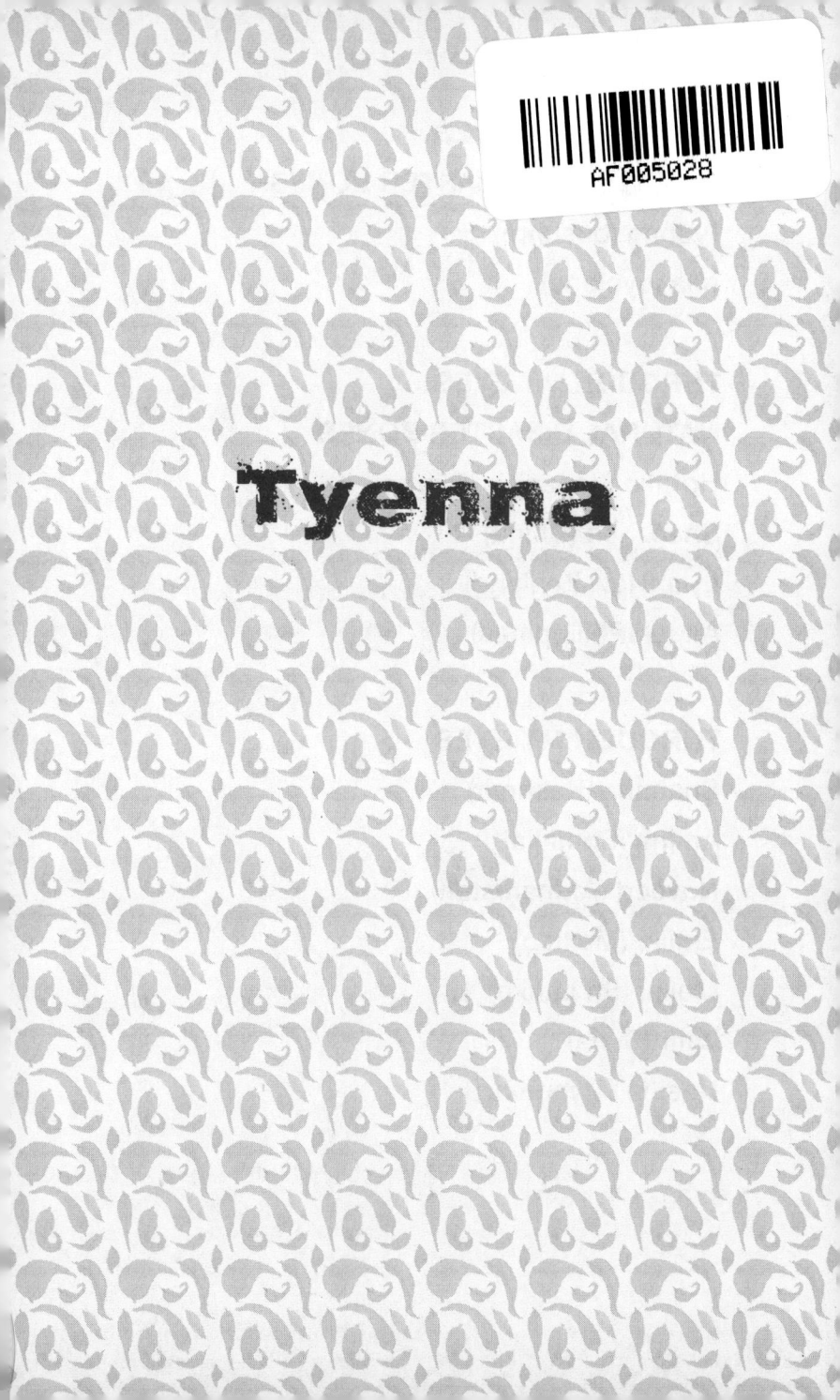

THROUGH MY EYES
AUSTRALIAN DISASTER ZONES
Tyenna (bushfire)
Mia (cyclone)

THROUGH MY EYES
NATURAL DISASTER ZONES
Hotaka (Japan)
Shaozhen (China)
Lyla (New Zealand)
Angel (Philippines)

THROUGH MY EYES
Shahana (Kashmir)
Amina (Somalia)
Naveed (Afghanistan)
Emilio (Mexico)
Malini (Sri Lanka)
Zafir (Syria)
Hasina (Myanmar)

THROUGH MY EYES AUSTRALIAN DISASTER ZONES

series editor Lyn White

Tyenna

JULIE HUNT and TERRY WHITEBEACH

ALLEN&UNWIN
SYDNEY·MELBOURNE·AUCKLAND·LONDON

First published by Allen & Unwin in 2022

Copyright © Julie Hunt and Terry Whitebeach, 2022
Series concept © series creator and editor Lyn White 2022

All rights reserved. No part of this book may be reproduced or transmitted in any form or by any means, electronic or mechanical, including photocopying, recording or by any information storage and retrieval system, without prior permission in writing from the publisher. The Australian *Copyright Act 1968* (the Act) allows a maximum of one chapter or ten per cent of this book, whichever is the greater, to be photocopied by any educational institution for its educational purposes provided that the educational institution (or body that administers it) has given a remuneration notice to the Copyright Agency (Australia) under the Act.

Allen & Unwin
83 Alexander Street
Crows Nest NSW 2065
Australia
Phone: (61 2) 8425 0100
Email: info@allenandunwin.com
Web: www.allenandunwin.com

A catalogue record for this book is available from the National Library of Australia

ISBN 978 1 76087 701 9

For teaching resources, explore www.allenandunwin.com/resources/for-teachers

Cover and text design by Sandra Nobes
Cover and text images: Girl by Juris Teivans / Alamy Stock Photo; pencil pines by Daniela Brozek; flames by PrasongTakham / Shutterstock; gum leaves pattern by Namartsy / Dreamstime
Set in 11/15 pt Plantin by Midland Typesetters, Australia
This book was printed in December 2021 by McPherson's Printing Group, Australia.

10 9 8 7 6 5 4 3 2 1

The paper in this book is FSC® certified.
FSC® promotes environmentally responsible, socially beneficial and economically viable management of the world's forests.

This story takes place in lutruwita/Tasmania on Big River Country. We acknowledge the traditional owners of this land, the palawa people, who belong to the oldest continuing culture in the world and who cared for and protected Country for thousands of years. We honour them and pay our respects to their elders, past, present and emerging.

The novel is set during the bushfires that occurred in the Central Highlands of Tasmania in 2019. The characters and many of the locations are fictional, to protect the privacy of communities and individuals. We have also altered the details and the chronology of various events, for the sake of the story. For example, we compressed the time frame – the actual fires went for more than a month and involved multiple emergency evacuations. But the essential truths of the devastation caused by the bushfire remain.

During our research we received generous assistance and much factual information from Central Highlands' community members and from relevant voluntary and professional emergency services, including Tasmania Fire Service and State Emergency Service. We have endeavoured to represent this information accurately, but any errors we may have made are ours alone and are no reflection on the integrity and practices of these services.

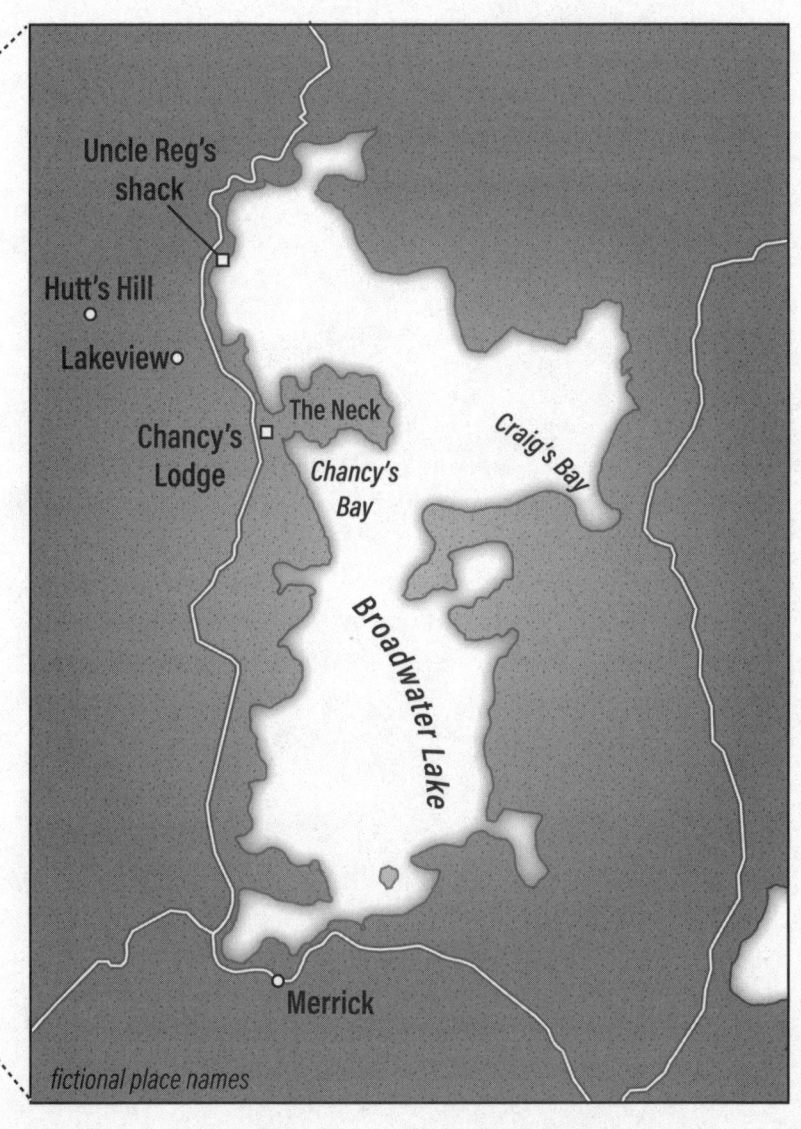

One

This is going to be her best holiday yet, Tyenna thinks, as she and Nan head out of the Launceston airport towards the Central Highlands.

It's summer. Tye's turning thirteen, she's back in Tasmania and her lovely pop is waiting to see her. He's promised her a big walk this year, a three-day trek into the Walls of Jerusalem. And her best friend Lily's bursting with plans for their time together. Plenty of things to look forward to.

As they turn off the highway and head towards Poatina, the Great Western Tiers loom ahead, reaching for the sky. Tye puts her head out the window. The air is so different from Melbourne. Soon they pass fields of dry stubble and Tye can see the pipeline glinting silver, way up high. Then they're climbing, weaving their way up to the plateau, Tye's favourite place. Chancy's Bay is just an hour and a half from Launceston but it seems a world away.

This is the fourth year in a row she's visited Nan and Pop. She loved the winter holidays with snow and roaring winds and the occasional still day when everything sparkled. And now she's here in summer. Nan and Pop are always glad to have her stay. So what's causing a worry wrinkle between Nan's eyebrows? And why is she so uncharacteristically silent?

'Is anything wrong, Nan?' Tye says at last.

Nan sighs. 'Sorry, sweetie, one or two things on my mind.'

'Such as?'

'In short, the weather. We had a shower a couple of days ago. One point two mil in the rain gauge, but that's all we've had so far this month. If this keeps up it'll be the driest January on record. Everyone's worried about fires.' Nan frowns. 'I'm afraid this might not turn out to be the carefree holiday you're expecting, Tye. For starters, Pop and I have to be at a community meeting in Merrick this afternoon.'

Tye tries to swallow her disappointment. She's good at taking things in her stride. But this wasn't what she planned for her first day.

'It's a pity,' Nan says. 'But your pop was called out to a blaze down near Lake Sorell even before Christmas and the fire service is flat out telling people to get their fire plans in place, especially the shack owners. Your grandad and the local fire crew are part of it, of course, along with us hall volunteers. Kay'll be chairing the meeting.'

'Kay? What about Pop?' For as long as Tye can remember, her pop has been fire chief.

'He thought it was time to hand over to Kay. She's a dynamo as you know and twenty years younger than us.'

Now it's Tye's turn to be silent, as she thinks over what Nan's said. She's been counting on having fun with Lily this summer after the slog of first year high school. And she can't wait for the walk with Pop. They're going to Dixon's Kingdom, that special place where the pencil pines – some more than a thousand years old – have been growing for over one hundred and fifty million years. She's been looking forward to it for months.

Her heart drops. Maybe the big walk won't happen after all?

They've nearly reached the top. Tye looks behind her, a breathtaking view across farmland to Ben Lomond. Ahead is a scree slope and then they're over the lip of the plateau and heading southwest. Tye puts aside her disappointment. She can't help feeling exhilarated. The big skies up here do it for her every time.

'Tell you what,' Nan says, her voice reverting to its usual cheery can-do tone, 'why don't we go straight to Pine Lake for a quick visit? We can pick up Lily en route. That way you get to see your best friend and your beloved trees first thing.'

'Great! I'd love that, Nan.'

'Send her a text. She's dying to see you.'

There's rocky terrain and scrabbled bush all the way to Merrick, the main settlement in the Highlands, at the southern end of Broadwater Lake. It has a couple of sealed roads with houses, a shop and service station behind the pub and a row of shacks along the foreshore.

They go straight through Merrick and follow the road north across tussocky plains, passing the fisheries and the Parks and Wildlife station. At the turnoff to Chancy's Bay Tye sees swirling clouds of dust and wonders. Nan drives on without comment.

Lily's waiting at her gate right next to the sign she made in primary school – *Lakeview*, the letters burnt into a pine plank. She's dancing with impatience.

'Tye!' Lily shrieks, and hurls herself at her friend. Then she pulls back and scans Tye, head to toe. 'Cute hairdo,' she comments. 'Suits you shorter. The streak looks super trendy.'

'Mum took me to her hairdresser as a Christmas treat.'

'Ni-ice,' Lily says. 'But no good for us dancers; we have to keep our hair long.' She shakes her fair curls. 'And I swear you've grown a metre since last year. My friend the giraffe!'

Tye grins. It's true – she's nearly as tall as her mother, Opal.

'You'll be amazed when I show you my new dance moves,' Lily says. 'Spectacular!'

The two girls chat excitedly.

'And they say I can talk!' Nan says, as she pulls up ten minutes later at Pine Lake. 'You two never draw breath.'

The air is cool and fresh. They set off, Nan in the lead, her footsteps heavy on the timber walkway. Solid is the best way to describe Nan: big capable hands and strong legs. Sun glinting on her grey-blonde hair as she turns to the girls. 'Don't dawdle.'

Lily runs ahead, stopping now and then to strike a pose, but Tye pauses at the first interpretation board.

This easy walk takes only about 30 mins return, but it may take you back over 100 million years.

Walking along between the pines, Tye imagines herself deep in Gondwanaland's ancient forests, among the pines with their rough bark, sculpted forms, dense green foliage, and life spans longer than humans can imagine.

'Thanks, Nan,' Tye says when they scramble back into the ute, cheeks and fingers tingling. 'That was the best.'

They drop Lily back at her gate, the two friends vowing to get together again at the earliest possible moment.

'You're going to be so excited when you see your—'

'Lily!' Nan says.

Lily giggles. 'Call me!' she shouts as the ute takes off.

As they turn in past the Chancy's Bay sign, Tye gasps. What meets her eyes is not the familiar tumble of buildings that make up Chancy's Lodge, her grandparents' holiday accommodation business nestled in the bush by Broadwater Lake, but chainsaws, a bulldozer and clouds of choking dust above piles of broken vegetation.

The grounds look like a tornado has hit. Felled trees and piles of branches lie in untidy heaps, and the parking area's rutted and churned.

'Rob!' Nan shouts over the noise of the bulldozer. 'Your granddaughter's here!'

Pop turns, his usual half smile becoming a broad grin. When he sees the look of dismay on Tye's face he hurries over and puts his arm around her. He's skinnier than Nan, shorter too. 'I know, chicken,' he says, 'but it had to be done. The bushfire risk is too great this year. I'll clear things up as soon as I get the firebreak in.'

Tye snuggles into his shoulder, feeling the rough texture of his shirt, and breathes in the familiar scent of eucalypt, fresh air, soil and sweat. He hugs her tight then steps back.

'You go and get yourself settled,' he tells her. 'Have a yarn with Nan while I get on with this. Have to make sure we're safe before those scorching northerlies get here. The bush is dry as tinder.'

He pats Tye's shoulder. 'By the way, sorry about our trip to the Walls. I can't get away right now.'

Another bad surprise. Will there be more? As if in answer, Pop says, 'Can't be helped, chicken. There'll be other times.'

Tye trails after her grandmother, who's moving at her usual rapid pace. But she's abruptly halted when a wombat comes hurtling along and nearly bowls her over. It's Myrtle. She's been at Chancy's as long as Tye can remember.

'Lance!' Nan calls. 'Come and take charge of this furry cannonball.'

A bearded old man in a cloth hat adorned with fishing flies approaches. 'Hello there, Opal,' he says when he spots Tye.

'Tyenna,' she corrects. 'My mum is Opal.'

Lance peers at Tye. 'Well, so it is!' he says, shaking his head. He takes off his thick glasses and cleans them with a grubby handkerchief.

Tye's shocked by the change a year has brought. There's something blurry about him. How old is Lance? Maybe a hundred?

'Now what's the problem, Lena?' he asks, putting his glasses back on and gazing vaguely at Tye's grandmother. *The lenses are so smeared it's a wonder he can see anything,* Tye thinks.

'This creature! Get her out of my hair right now – or else!'

Tye smiles to herself. Some things never change. Nan's been at war with Myrtle forever. And Myrtle's still winning, in spite of being nearly blind and well past her twentieth birthday. Nan keeps threatening to get rid of the old wombat if Lance can't keep her under control, but Tye knows that'll never happen. Myrtle's as much part of the Chancy's family as Lance – she's always been there, just like the old man.

'Gotta get back to my fly-tying,' Lance mutters. 'Come on, Myrtle.' And they both bumble off.

Nan shakes her head. 'Cup of tea,' she says to Tye, 'then we'll get you organised.'

Over tea and Anzac biscuits Nan asks about everyone at home. 'How's it working out with Opal and Jasmine? Getting used to having another mum?'

Tye nods. 'Jas's great. She's much more organised than Mum. My sports gear's always ready on PE days.'

Nan laughs.

'She works at the ABC, you know. She's worked there for years.'

'Good for her,' Nan says, then, a shade too casually, 'Opal see you off, then?'

'Jas did. She got time off. Mum's in Queensland, trying out for a new film role.'

Nan's face says it all. Time to change the subject.

'How much does Pop have to clear?' Tye asks.

'Just the bush between the road and the carpark.'

'Not the snow gums?'

'No, they're safe for now. But it's shaping up to be a grim summer for fires.'

That worry-crease deepens between Nan's eyes. 'Come on, now,' she says, rising from the table, 'let's get you set up.'

Nan follows Tye outside. Tye grabs her pack from the ute and is heading back towards the house and the curtained-off space in the hallway she uses as a bedroom when Nan says, 'Not that way. Around the side.'

Tye's grandmother gives a mysterious smile. 'I've got another surprise. A good one, this time.'

Near the back door Tye sees a covered walkway. 'That's new,' she says, 'and, look, you've moved one of the cabins close to the house.'

Nan leads her to the cabin and throws open the door. 'It's for you!'

Tye gasps. A place of her own, freshly painted.

'Pop's work,' Nan says, 'with help from Lance and Myrtle, of course. He built the walkway and shifted the cabin. Lily helped choose the colours. Pale blue for the walls, forest green for the shelves. Thought we'd never get it finished in time.'

The blobs of colour on Nan's sleeves had given Tye a clue, but she couldn't have imagined anything as good as this cool, quiet, uncluttered space, just for her. And overlooking the lake. Well, not exactly overlooking it, but allowing enticing glimpses through the scrub. And a good view of the rest of Chancy's through its glass door. The restful blue of the walls, the new shelves waiting for her belongings and above the bed, a Wilderness Society poster of pencil pines . . . Tye is speechless with delight.

'You're growing up,' Nan says, giving her a hug. 'Getting too big for that curtained-off cubby in the hallway. I'll give you a few moments to settle in but then we have to be off. Don't worry, you'll have the rest of the summer to enjoy it.'

Twenty minutes later they're in Merrick.

Fire chief Kay greets them at the door of the community hall. She's still in her work uniform from the pub.

'Hey Tye, welcome back. We're looking for a fullback for the local team. Can we recruit you?'

Tye grins. Kay plays centre half-forward, the hardest position. She's a legend at marking and kicking goals.

Sleek as a greyhound and twice as fast, Tye's heard Kay's teammates say. *And a good people handler, too, she'd have to be, working at the pub.*

In minutes Kay's mustered the milling group and got the meeting underway. She urges people to read the fire readiness leaflets on their chairs, to look at the checklist. Ask themselves whether they have trees growing over their roofs, gutters full of leaves. Clear a thirty-five-metre firebreak around their residence.

'Everybody should have their bushfire plan in place by now,' she says.

Bushfire plan? Tye doesn't like the sound of that.

'Everyone thinks it won't happen to them,' Kay continues. 'I was speaking to a woman yesterday and I thought I was getting through, when she said, *Listen Kay, I think I'll give it a miss. I wouldn't know where to begin.* I told her she could move the woodheap for a start. It was stacked against the wall.'

People laugh, but a ripple of unease spreads through the hall.

'Check your insurance policy,' Kay reminds them. 'Make sure you're covered.'

Tye scans the headings on a bushfire preparation leaflet: *make a fire plan; clear your property; prepare an emergency kit; know when to leave and where to go; check ABC local radio and TFS website; monitor the weather.*

Her uneasiness grows. This is all well outside her experience. Bushfires have been something on the news up till now. She glances at Nan, then at Pop. Their serious expressions do nothing to reassure her.

Two

The morning is chilly as it often is in the Highlands, even in January. Tye pulls up the doona and looks out the window. Mist is rising from the water. Maybe she and Lil will go out in the kayaks.

She checks her phone. Jas has left a message.

Happy first day of being thirteen! Wishing you a wonderful day. Hope you like the present. Your mum chose it. Give you a call tonight. xxx

There's a message from Lukas, Tye's friend from the science club at school. He doesn't know it's her birthday.

Hey Tye. Missed you at the climate meeting last night. Heaps there. Greta Thunberg doesn't know what she's started. Keep 15 March free. Lots to do before then. Come back soon. Love to Tassie. Love to the planet.

No text from Opal yet. *Bit early for Mum*, Tye thinks. *She'll probably call me later.*

She gets up and goes to the door. It's busy outside. Walkers are packing up near the cabins, their gear laid out on the ground. A young couple sit at the picnic table, eating breakfast, a map spread out before them. Lance is at work already, his card table set up on the veranda outside his room. He's wearing some odd sort of headgear with a glass visor and a magnified loop. There's a row of headlights across his forehead. Tye can't help laughing.

She slips on her clothes and is about to run over to say good morning to him when Lily calls her on the phone, launching straight into a heartfelt rendition of 'Happy Birthday' accompanied by much panting and thumping. She's doing her routine to the song and it sounds strenuous.

'... birthday toooo yooooooou'...!' The last note dies away and Lily says, 'Now I'm in full splits.'

Tye falls about laughing. 'Thanks, Lil. Do it again tonight?'

'At the party? No way. Have a great day, Tye.'

'How about we go out on the lake?'

'Can't. Rehearsal this morning and I'm ... ah ... busy this arvo.'

Tye knows she's meant to ask what her friend's doing, but she doesn't get the chance.

'Not saying. But you'll see soon enough. Bye!'

Tye opens the gift Jas gave her at the airport. A beautiful silk scarf. She reads the tag: *Hand-dyed from Eucalyptus leaves.* Puts the scarf on and heads over to Lance. He sees her coming and raises his hand.

'Can't talk, Tyenna. It's mail day and I've got an order to fill.'

Tye steps up on the veranda. 'Myrtle about?'

'Inside.' Lance looks up and almost blinds Tye with the beam of his headlights. 'She had a bad night.'

The door's open so Tye peeks into his room. There's a huge bump in the middle of the bed.

'Lance, she's in your bed!'

'It happens,' he says. 'Get my pliers, will you? They should be on the bench.'

Lance's room looks more like a workshop than a bedroom. Tye finds the pliers on top of a fishing box full of feathers, fur, hooks, beads and reels of shiny coloured thread – the materials he uses for his flies.

Lance takes the pliers and mumbles his thanks. He holds up what appears to be a tiny grey insect with silver wings. It glitters in the light.

'I once bagged a ten-pound brown with one of these.'

'Trout?'

He switches off his lights, lifts his visor and focuses on Tye. 'What else? Where have you been?' Then he returns to his work. 'Tell your pop I won't be long. Just one more to go.'

Tye smells eggs and bacon. She heads back to the walkway and makes her way to her grandparents' porch, pausing at the screen door.

'Queensland,' Nan is saying. 'She's in Queensland. *Surely* you'd think—'

'Just leave it, darl,' Pop says. 'Are those boys in Snowgum staying another night?'

'Ask Lance. He seems to be running the place. After a fashion! He's double-booked again this week.' Tye hears Nan sigh. 'I can't seem to get through to him.'

It seems like Nan isn't in the best of moods. But when Tye kicks off her boots, her grandmother turns, all smiles. She kisses Tye on both cheeks.

'Happy birthday, love. Do you want your present now or will we wait for the party tonight?'

'Tonight. And, Nan, you've already given me a present.' Tye still can't quite believe the cabin is hers.

'So what are you going to do till then?'

Tye shrugs. 'Not sure yet.'

'How about coming with me on the mail run?' Pop suggests with a sideways look at Nan. 'I could use some help and your nan's got a bit on her plate today.' He gives Tye a wink.

'Sounds good to me,' she says.

A short time later they're in the van, heading down to Bothwell, an hour away. A box of fishing flies is on Tye's lap, addressed to someone in America, in Lance's shaky writing.

'How's your mum?' Pop asks as the van bounces along the gravel road.

'She's good, Pop. She reckons she might get this film job in Queensland.'

'Going to crack the big one, eh?'

'Maybe.' Tye gives him a smile. She doesn't have to worry with Pop. No need to defend her mum or try to cover up for her. 'Guess it could happen one day.'

'Who knows? But what about you? So grown up. A year's a long time, eh?'

'Jas says to say hello. She'd like to meet you.'

'That'd be good. She's welcome anytime. They both are.'

They pass through Merrick. From there the road to Bothwell crosses windswept plains before descending from the plateau, winding through more gentle bush and farmland. They pass the stone gatepost of Studleyvale, Pop's family sheep property.

'Look at the paddocks,' he says. 'Never been so dry. Not even a green pick near the river. Your great-auntie Jill will be feeding out by the end of the month if this keeps up.'

A few kilometres on and they're in the township. Sandstone church, old cottages, a stock and station agent, and the hunting shop with a deer's head in the window. They park outside the post office. The day's getting hotter. Tye dispatches Lance's parcel and Pop collects the mail.

Then they leave Bothwell and weave their way back up through the Highlands, stopping at roadside mailboxes, sometimes for a brief chat, sometimes just to stuff letters into old milk churns, breadboxes, dented 44-gallon drums, whatever passes as a letterbox for the various drop-off points and homesteads on the mail run. Whenever there's a box her grandfather can't reach from the window, or a parcel to retrieve from the back, Tye jumps out. Pop thanks her for her help.

Soon they're back in Merrick.

'That's just about it,' Pop says, 'except for the Hermit of Hutt's Hill. We're not really meant to home deliver, but Barry's a special case.'

He takes the mail into the shop and returns with a single letter. And they're off again, over the plains beyond the settlement, heading for Chancy's.

'Want me to drop you off?'

Tye shakes her head. She's enjoying the ride, and the time alone with Pop.

They pass Chancy's and Tye sees that the bulldozer has gone, along with the heaps of rubbish. It looks better than yesterday, just an ordinary mess rather than a war zone. They pass Lily's place and a few minutes further on Pop turns up a rutted track to a locked and bolted gate. A cacophony of barking greets them.

'I'm not getting out here,' Tye says, as two black streaks hurtle out of the bush and fling themselves at the gate, snarling and foaming.

'They're fine once you get to know them,' Pop reassures her. 'No problem at all as long as you stay on this side of the fence, though the word is their bite is worse than their bark.'

'Barry!' he roars up the hill. 'It's Rob! All right, mate? Mail!'

The answer is a single rifle shot, which splits the air and makes Tye's ears ring.

'Friendly fire,' Pop reassures her. 'Just Barry's way of saying g'day.'

He puts the letter in the box and backs down the track. 'Barry lost a close friend not long ago, so we're keeping an eye on him. Seems to be okay, so far. Your nan came up the other day.'

'She went past those dogs?'

'It would take more than a couple of mastiffs to put your grandmother off.'

As they turn back onto the main road, Tye spots something moving in the bush. A wallaby, perhaps? No, it's too big for a wallaby. It dives out of sight before she can get a proper look. Through the scrub she can just make out the lake. Then she sees something bobbing in the bushes – a yellow hat.

'A boy,' she says, pointing. 'Down there.'

'Don't reckon,' says Pop. 'There's nothing down that way except old Reg Stokes' place. It's empty now.' He turns on the radio. Nothing interesting, just the weather report and updates on fires around the state. Tye looks back into the bush. It *is* a boy. Peeping out from behind a tree. He's looking right at her. Then he turns and runs.

The party that night is terrific, much better than being in Melbourne with Opal away and Jas working till late. Lily's wearing a lime green halter-neck frock that Nan swears is the one she wore to the first Longford Folk Festival.

'RSPCA op shop in Deloraine,' Lily announces.

She's brought her mum, Carla, the local wildlife carer, who has three joeys in her shoulder bag, all of which need feeding.

'We left Dad to do the rest,' Lil says. Lily is so used to feeding baby creatures she can almost do it in her sleep.

'Welcome back, Tye,' Carla says, handing both girls a joey and a bottle. 'It's just like old times.'

Tye stares at the third little creature Carla takes from the bag. 'A devil, is it?'

Carla nods. 'Imp. Three months old and going well.' She passes the teat under the devil's shiny black nose then pops it in his mouth. He sucks greedily.

Once the animals are fed it's time for the cake. Lily made it and she doesn't hide her pride.

She holds the platter above her head. 'It's called a Persian love cake. What do you think?' Three layers high and iced with cream that's dotted with crystallised flower petals, the cake takes Tye's breath away. And it tastes as good as it looks.

'Thanks, Lil,' she cries. 'Did it take all afternoon?'

'I did the petals yesterday,' Lil says. 'I can teach you how.' She lowers her voice. 'I've got something else for you too. Show you later.'

Lance gives Tye a delicately wrought fishing fly, fashioned into a brooch, and Nan and Pop give her a sleeping bag, superfine down.

'For your bushwalks,' Nan says.

'It's too much,' Tye tells her. 'You've already given me a cabin!'

'We've only got one granddaughter,' Pop says. 'And this should last you for years.'

Lily draws Tye into a quiet corner and opens out a large sheet of paper, covered in symbols and diagrams. 'It's an astrological chart,' she explains, in reply to Tye's dazed expression. 'A woman in Deloraine makes them into posters.'

Tye doesn't know how to respond. 'It's . . . kind of you, Lil,' she begins.

'It tells you everything you need to know for the next year.'

'Everything?' Tye echoes faintly.

'This is your sun sign, your moon and your rising. And these triangles here—'

'Maybe later when I have a good look at it, you could explain it a bit more.' Tye's down-to-earth mind is rebelling against this – what does Pop call it? Pseudoscience? but she doesn't want to hurt her friend's feelings. So she keeps her doubts to herself. She's good at doing that.

'Oh okay,' Lily says with obvious regret. 'But just look at this bit – it indicates a significant pledge which you must be sure not to break.'

'Right,' Tye says.

Then someone arrives whom Tye hasn't met before.

'This is Kelly-Ann,' Nan says. 'She's as fond of the pines as you are.'

The young woman is wearing a Parks uniform and holding a seedling in a pot. She's shorter than Tye and with her dimpled cheeks and her hair in a single plait, doesn't look much older. She's a ranger, Nan tells Tye.

'Sorry I didn't have time to wrap it.' Kelly-Ann fishes a tag from her pocket and pokes it in next to the plant. 'Happy Birthday.'

Tye reads the name, *Athrotaxis cupressoides*.

'A pencil pine! Thank you. How old is it?'

'Just three years. You'll need to live a long time to see it grow much. What is it – a metre every fifty years? It's mates are back in the nursery,' she says, 'two thousand of them waiting to be planted out. A friend of mine is doing a research project.'

'What sort of research?'

'Tye, how about offering our guest a piece of cake?' Nan suggests.

Tye gets the cake and hurries back. Soon she and Kelly-Ann are deep in conversation.

'I've always had a thing for them,' Kelly-Ann says. 'When I was little I used to draw them with dinosaurs.'

Tye smiles at the thought.

'Trouble is they're not regenerating like they used to.'

Kelly-Ann takes out her phone and shows Tye a picture that looks like fairyland. A forest of pencil pines, with bright green moss in the foreground and water streaming over a rock wall behind.

'That was my favourite place until three years ago. Now I can barely look at it.'

She swipes to the next picture. Brown moss, blackened rocks and burnt trees. 'Lost a lot of pines in that fire. They won't grow back. This is where we'll do the plantings.' She swipes her phone again. Bone-white trunks flash past, stands of skeleton trees stark against the sky.

'Some of these are from earlier fires, decades ago. They're part of the story too, the stags. That's what we call the dead ones.' She turns to Tye. 'Hey, you might like to help when we start planting out.'

'I'd love to!'

When Jas's promised call comes through, Tye wanders to the door, talking. The evening is still hot and there are flashes of lightning over the distant hills.

'Fireworks for the girl's birthday,' Lance says when Tye returns.

Kelly-Ann frowns. 'I hope not.'

Then the buzzer at the front of the house sounds.

'That'll be the Swiss backpackers,' Nan says. 'Better late than never.'

Meanwhile Pop's fiddling with the laptop from the office. 'Tye, how do you connect this to the TV? Your nan had it set up earlier. It was working before—'

Suddenly an enormous picture of five-year-old Tye appears on the screen.

Pop leaps aside. 'Whoa, here's trouble!' Everyone laughs.

'Now for the formal part of the evening,' Nan says as she returns. 'The slide show!'

It's a bit embarrassing: a younger Tye shaking her finger at Myrtle, who hasn't changed a bit. Tye riding a little tricycle outside Lance's room on the veranda of the accommodation block that had started life as the singlemen's quarters in one of the early Hydro villages.

Then Tye as a baby in Opal's arms down near the boat ramp.

'That was just after you were born,' Nan says. 'The morning Opal brought you home from the Launceston General.'

Another of Opal in sunglasses, striking a pose, one hand behind her head, eyes cast skywards.

'She's a Leo for sure,' Lily says. 'Look at that mane.'

Then one of Opal and Tye in the shearing shed at Studleyvale. Tye's five years old and holding a lamb.

'Remember Lucy?' Pop asks. 'That was the year before you left Tassie.'

Tye nods. She wonders if Lucy's still on the farm.

The next photo shows Tye on Pop's knee in the fire truck with the rest of the crew. Kay's there, looking younger. The truck's festooned with Christmas decorations and the siren must be going because Tye's squealing with delight. Then there's a picture of her great grandparents, Nan's mum and dad, Olga and Josef Zabowski – a really old one, in the Hydro camp where they used to work when they first arrived from Poland. 'That's Opal's babcia,' Nan says, 'your prababcia – great grandmother.'

Pretty soon it's time for Carla and Lily to get back home for the next round of feeds. And Kelly-Ann needs to go too.

'It was a great party, thank you so much,' Tye tells Nan and Pop, as they pile the dishes and glasses onto the kitchen bench.

Tye goes to her new room and puts her seedling on the bedside table. She takes a photo of it, then unzips the sleeping bag and spreads it on the bed.

Satisfied, she lies down, savouring the evening, gazing out at the star-filled sky. That's something she's always loved about the Highlands, the huge night skies, with the stars wheeling above. She wonders briefly about the mysterious pledge in Lily's astrological chart, then settles to sleep.

A thought intrudes. *Promises*. That's it. The one tiny gap in her happiness. Opal hasn't called. She's forgotten her only daughter's birthday. She'd promised too. But that's Opal. Promises don't mean much to her.

Three

Nan's busy making patties when Tye comes in for breakfast next morning. A bread-and-butter pudding in an ovenproof dish is sitting on the counter.

'Are we having visitors?' Tye asks.

'No, we're invited to Ted and Pearlie's, down near Brady's Lake, for morning tea, and I thought I'd whip up a few things to leave with them for later.'

'Do I know them?'

'Maybe not. Old mates of Lance's – and of Pop's for that matter. He and Jill have known them since they were kids. Ted used to work for Pop's father. They're getting on a bit. Thought we'd see how they're doing.'

'Okay, I'll go over to Lily's and see if she wants to come too,' Tye says, and before Nan can reply, she's out the door. She raises the seat on her nan's old blue bike, pumps up the tyres and pedals fast to Lakeview. She's there in twenty minutes, which must be a record. 'Lil, Lil!' she calls, propping the bike against the veranda rail.

But Lily isn't there. The house is closed up and the curtains drawn. Then Tye remembers Lily's dance rehearsal in Deloraine. She won't be back in time. Disappointed, Tye turns the bike around, wheels it down the drive and heads back home.

It's not until she gets there that she realises she no longer has her phone. She searches her pockets. Nothing. It must have bounced out somewhere between Lakeview and Chancy's.

'Nan,' she wails. 'My phone. I've lost it. I have to go back and look for it.'

'No time,' Nan says. 'I told Pearlie we'd be there by eleven. You know how some people are about punctuality. Anyway, you can manage without your phone for a few hours.' Then, seeing Tye's crestfallen expression, she adds, 'Don't worry. No one uses that track except you and Lily. The phone'll still be there when we get back, you'll see. We can go over and look for it later.' Then she adds, 'I take it Lily had other plans.'

'Another dance rehearsal.'

Pop bundles Lance into the car and hands Tye the box of supplies to nurse. Down the familiar road towards Merrick, then south-west across the plateau. It's a warm day and the breeze sends bush scents wafting into the vehicle. Tye sets the worry about her phone aside and listens to Pop reminiscing about when he and Jill were kids and rode their ponies up to the high pastures with their family's flocks every summer.

'Ted was a great shepherd,' Pop tells Tye.

'The best,' Lance comments. 'Nearly as good a shepherd as I am a fisherman.'

Pop gives a snort of laughter. 'Perhaps a touch more modest.'

'And Pearl was a dab hand at shepherding in her day, too, wasn't she?' Nan adds.

'She was,' Pop replies, 'and a wonderful rider.'

When they arrive, Ted's at the woodpile, wielding an axe. A stringy old man, bent-backed but looking as tough as the mountain gums that thrive in all weathers in the high country. The woodheap is enormous. He waves his hat as Pop draws to a stop. An old woman, as stringy and bent as her husband, appears at the door of a modest cottage.

'Right on cue,' she calls. 'The kettle's on the boil and the scones are just out of the oven. Come in, come in.'

The men shake hands. Nan introduces Tye. 'My granddaughter, Tyenna. She's staying with us for the holidays.'

'That right?' the woman says. 'Pleased to meet you, Tyenna. That old feller's Ted. I'm Pearl. Known your grandad since he was knee high to a grasshopper. And your nan's people as well, when they could barely speak a word of English. Hard workers they were, too.'

'Like you,' Pop says.

'Not these days,' Ted replies. 'Pretty much take it easy.'

'Not by the look of your woodpile.'

'Feller's got to have something to occupy himself with. No good sitting round all day studying yourself.'

'How have you been keeping?' Pop says, as Nan sets down the box of goodies they've brought. Tye looks around curiously. It's an old-fashioned room, pine dresser, laminex table, wooden bench with a mincer attached to one end, fuel stove, pictures from calendars on the walls. It's like stepping back in time.

'Fair to middling,' Pearl replies.

'At this stage we're on the wrong side of everything,' Ted adds. 'Still, as long as we stay on the right side of the grass, that's all that matters.'

He speaks loudly as if he's shouting over a crowd.

'Old age is not for the faint-hearted,' Lance says, in such grim tones they all laugh.

'The old girl's been on at me to go to the doctor's to get me ears blown out. But why bother? I can hear what I need to. And for the rest I just listen to the land. It tells me all I need to know. It's just a matter of paying attention.'

They tuck in; the scones are tasty and the teapot is refilled twice before they all declare themselves well fed and watered. Lance has dozed off, Nan and Pearl are talking knitting patterns and Ted takes Pop off to his shed.

Tye's gazing at a row of crocheted egg-cosies on the dresser and idly wondering what Ted means by listening to the land, when Pearl says, 'Go for a bit of a wander if you like, youngster. Take Nimble with you.'

A bright-eyed kelpie sits to attention, looking eager. Tye unlatches the flywire door and steps out. Nimble dances around her, wagging his tail. The air is fresh and spicy. Currawongs call, and smaller birds peep and twitter. There's a sense of quietness, of things being right, in this out-of-the-way place. And a sweet citrus scent.

Cider gums in flower. Pop had pointed them out to her yesterday on the mail run and explained why they were called that.

'First Nations people used to travel all over the plateau. Big River Country they called it, and in summer they made a drink from the sap. Supposed to be delicious. Never tried it myself, but. Wonderful trees, but unlike most eucalypts, they don't recover after bushfires.'

Tye wanders a bit further, passing clumps of rushes and white flax iris. There's so much to see, so much to learn and understand. She peers up into the trees from time to time, searching for knot-holes, wondering which ones hold possums curled up sound asleep. Then she finds a grassy spot and sits down. The ground is rock hard. Maybe it's always like this in summer. When she hears a high-pitched call she scans the branches, finally sees something flicker in the foliage, then a bright metallic flash as the bird takes flight. She wonders what it was. Ted would know. He's half deaf but he listens to the country, probably reads it like a book. Tye wishes she could do that. How long would it take to learn? Perhaps a lifetime.

A sharp breeze springs up, as if in answer, and with it, a yearning. If only she could understand what the land is telling her, discern what the wind is saying. She stands stock still, listening, looking, letting the wind tickle her neck. The breeze through the leaves above makes a rushing sound like water.

No wonder Ted and Pearl have lived here their whole lives, she thinks.

There's a timeless feel to the bush, something that makes you feel strong and grounded. She's hungry for knowledge of how to keep it that way, slow down global warming, help fight climate change, make sure the land remains healthy. Maybe she can learn. Maybe she can be part of it.

When Tye returns to the house, talk has turned, unsurprisingly, to bushfires.

'The trouble is, country's so overgrown,' Ted's saying. 'Things were better before this became a protected area. When we were still grazing cattle up there and hunting and trapping.'

'It was a good life,' Pearl adds.

'And the cattle and sheep kept the fuel load at bay,' Ted says, 'but look at it now. There are places where you can't get through the undergrowth. And the kerosene bush; fire spreads through it faster than you can blink.' He chuckles. 'Mother's jumper the old trappers used to call it. When the snow was deep they'd set it alight to keep themselves warm. We followed the way Aboriginal people did it. From way back they used fire to create pasture for the kangaroo and wallaby; we did the same for the stock. Before all this heritage stuff locked the land up.'

'Contentious ground you're venturing onto here,' Pop comments mildly.

'It's about looking after the land, managing it for the long term,' Ted says, 'like the Aborigines did for millennia. We haven't done so well since then.'

Pop and Ted start talking about the big fire, in 1967, which spread throughout the island. Rob was only a kid then. More than sixty people died, as well as thousands of animals, and great swathes of bush were destroyed. People were left homeless. Was this a one-off or an indication of what everyone's started to call the new normal? Tye's been hearing that a lot the last year or so. But where's everything heading? She dreads to think. She wonders what Lukas and his climate strikers are planning next.

'We've had disasters before, haven't we?' she says, thinking of the planet being hit by meteors, wobbling off its axis, volcanos filling the seas with bubbling lava, ice ages, droughts, the continents splitting apart.

'They seem to be getting more frequent,' Ted says. 'And we humans have made some pretty big blues.'

'Ted, stop upsetting the girl,' Pearl interrupts. 'Try looking on the bright side. We've done some good things as well.'

As if on cue Lance sits bolt upright, blinking furiously. 'Best move they ever made, stocking the lakes with trout!'

Nan and Pop roar laughing, and Ted and Pearl join in.

'One track mind, old mate,' Ted says. 'Fishing's all you ever think about. You want to watch out the Broadwater bunyip doesn't get you.'

Tye feels confused. This old couple obviously love the bush and yet they seem to be disagreeing with government protection and conservationists. Where would her pencil pines be if cattle and sheep were allowed to graze on them? She determines to speak to Pop about it later. And what's this bunyip?

Lance seems unfazed. 'I don't worry about things like that. Anyway, no one's caught sight of it in the last sixty years. And as long as it doesn't kill the fish, I'd say let sleeping bunyips lie.'

Everyone laughs again. Pearl points at the teapot. Nan shakes her head.

'Time we made tracks,' Pop says, getting to his feet. 'Anything we can do for you before we go?'

'Thanks mate, but we're pretty right,' Ted says, struggling up out of his chair. 'Our new neighbours lend a hand when we need it. They're only a kilometre away.'

Pearl smiles. 'Climate refugees they call themselves. From the mainland.'

'More of them moving to the plateau every day,' Ted adds. 'Got some pretty rum ideas, some of them, but they're good-hearted folk, generally speaking.'

Tye carries the empty food box out to the car.

'So you're not thinking of moving closer in?' Pop says as Ted leans on the wing mirror of their ute.

'No way,' Ted replies.

Pearl presses a hand-knitted knee rug into Tye's arms. 'For the nights. It can get pretty cold up here.'

Tye stammers her thanks, and Pop backs down the rutted driveway. Nimble chases the car to the turnoff.

Tye's quiet on the way home. The time at Ted and Pearl's has woken a hunger in her. A hunger for greater understanding of the bush, and for other things she finds hard to put into words.

Nan's phone interrupts her musings.

'For you,' Nan says, handing the phone to Tye. 'Lily.'

'Given up answering your own phone, have you?' comes Lily's voice.

'I came over to get you, this morning,' Tye says. 'To come with us to these friends of Pop's, but you weren't there.'

'Rehearsal. Deloraine. Did you forget?' Lily gives a mock groan. 'And now I've got about a thousand more sequins to sew on. But that doesn't explain why you won't answer your phone.'

'I lost it. Somewhere between Chancy's and Lakeview.'

'Bummer,' Lily replies. 'But, hey, no sweat, I'll help you look for it. Come over.'

'As soon as I get back. Thanks, Lil.'

'That'll be one you'll owe me,' Lily chirps and ends the call.

Four

Lily is waiting on her veranda, using the railing as a barre. She cups her heel in her hand and slowly straightens her leg until it's pointing skywards.

'Perfect timing,' she says. 'Mum's just about to start the next round of feeds. It's busy in the neonatal ward.'

'Too busy.' Carla appears at the door with a tray of little plastic bottles. 'Good to see you, Tye. Lovely party last night.' She waves and disappears into the house.

Lily drops her leg and takes Tye's hand. 'How was the visit?'

'Fine, Lil. Ted and Pearlie are pretty cool. Funny to think of people spending their whole life in the bush, though.'

'They're a blast from the past, those old timers, aren't they? My rehearsal was good too. I told Nicki about you.'

Lily drags Tye through the kitchen into the lounge room where Carla is waiting. It looks like a childcare centre. Wall-to-wall playpens, each one containing several creatures. Knitted pouches hang off the chairs and there's a washing basket on the floor full of little round wombats, all fast asleep. A small ringtail possum is climbing the flue cover above the wood heater, and before Tye can sit down, a joey bounces into her legs then bounds away.

'Bettong,' Lil says. 'Total nutcase. He always goes bonkers before a feed.'

Carla gently picks up the joey, wraps him in a cloth and hands him to Tye.

'Would you mind doing the honours?'

So Tye finds herself feeding one creature after another. The bettong, a baby bandicoot, two wallaby joeys, several wombats and a pademelon. She remembers the routine from last year – mixing formula, feeding, cleaning, and ticking each animal off on the chart Carla has up on the wall. Lily sits on the couch beside Tye, handling the joeys with casual competence.

'Can't stay till the end, Mum,' she says. 'We need to find Tye's phone.'

'Who's Nicki?' Tye asks, without looking up. She's marvelling at the tiny face in her hand. The baby is holding the teat with its paws and seems to be smiling, its eyes closed.

'New teacher,' says Lil. 'She said you're welcome to come to practice but she can't promise you'll be in the performance.'

Tye rolls her eyes. 'Lil, you know I don't—'

'You never know till you try. By the way I've got something to show you.'

Tye finishes feeding the joey and follows her friend into the bedroom. A new floor-to-ceiling mirror is fixed to one wall. The edges are draped with multicoloured scarves and a costume rack stands beside it. Lily's clothes are all over the floor, and the mirror doubles the chaos in her room.

'Wow, that's new,' Tye says.

'Dad got it for me. I'm paying him back. You wouldn't believe how many dreamcatchers I'll have to make for Candles and Crystals to pay for it. But that's not what I want to show you – it's these.' Lily pulls a sketchpad from a pile of books and magazines on her desk. She opens it at a page full of swirly drawings. 'Our costumes!' she declares.

'*Our* costumes?'

'Well, mine. I've had some brilliant ideas for yours too.'

'You're not serious?'

'Guess not,' says Lily with a wistful sigh. She pauses. 'You know, Tye, I was thinking after you left . . . maybe you *wanted* to lose your phone.'

'What? Why would I want to do that?'

'Because of your mum. She calls or she doesn't call. Either way, it's a problem.'

'Rubbish.'

'I still reckon that unconsciously you willed it to happen.'

Tye rolls her eyes. 'Come on, let's go find my phone.'

Lily nods. 'Bring our bathers as well?'

'Sure. As long as you have a spare pair I can use.'

'Always,' Lil says, stuffing things into a beach bag.

Tye dinks Lily down the drive and across the main road onto the track. Then they get off and walk, pushing the bike, and scanning the ground. No sign of the phone.

'I can't say it surprises me,' says Lil. 'It's Mercury retro and that always means communication problems.'

'So I lost my phone because of the planets?'

'Everything's connected,' Lily says, looking through the trees at the water.

It's almost evening and the lake has taken on a violet hue.

'Let's go for a dip. We can find the phone later.'

Tye shakes her head. She leans the bike against a stump, scanning the bushes at either side of the track. 'It could be anywhere,' she groans. 'My contact list. All my photos.' *And my messages*, she thinks. *Opal's probably remembered my birthday by now.*

Lily fishes her own phone out of the beach bag and holds it up triumphantly. 'Use this. Walk around and ring your number.'

'Genius! Thanks, Lil.'

Tye takes the phone but soon heaves a sigh. 'No battery.'

'What? I don't believe it!' Lily takes back her phone and stares at it accusingly. 'Flat. Zero. Zilch. How can that be?'

'Mercury retro, I guess,' Tye mutters.

'I'll go back and borrow Mum's.'

'It's okay, Lil. I'll get Nan's. I should be going home anyway. It's nearly teatime.'

'I bet you find it on the way. Swim tomorrow, then?'

'For sure.'

Tye drops Lily at the main road then heads back down the track, riding slowly and scanning the ground.

She doesn't find the phone. All she finds is Lance's hat, near Chancy's.

Pop and Nan have just finished dinner.

'Find it?' Nan asks, dishing out a plate for Tye.

'Not yet. I'll have a look later. Fish? Yay!'

'Lance caught it. He told me he was casting from the shallows, but I bet he was out on the lake again. I wish he wouldn't. Can you talk to him, Rob?'

'He won't take any notice,' Pop says.

'That's part of the problem,' Nan says.

Pop does not reply.

Tye sits down to her favourite meal. They hardly ever have fish at home. It's so expensive. And never as fresh as this.

'It was a good day, wasn't it,' Pop says. 'Not so much fun tomorrow. Property assessments with Kay. Trying to get people to wake up to themselves. The permanent residents are okay but it'll be hard going with the shack owners. Might have to take my tools and get people started.'

Tye eats quickly, then collects Nan's phone. It's light until late and she hopes she'll find the phone without too much trouble.

'Won't be long, Nan.' As she leaves she notices thunderheads banking over the hills behind Chancy's, great towering pillars of them. It might rain. Good for the country but bad for the phone.

After a while Tye puts down the bike, calls her number and listens. She hears leaves rustling in the breeze, the hoarse caw of a crow, but no phone. She walks ten paces and tries again, wishing she'd chosen a better ringtone than a silly tinkling star sound. That's more Lily's style. She needs something robust. Alarm or Bell Tower. She hears a car go past on the road, the drone of insects, a seed pod cracking open in the heat.

Another ten paces. She tries again, stands still, listens. Now there are two crows and they're hassling an eagle. She can hear the high-pitched cheeping. She looks up and sees them flying towards the lake, the eagle trying to gain height while the smaller birds attack it from above. She walks on and tries again. No luck.

Soon she's hearing the sound of birds settling for the night and scrabbling noises of small creatures in the bushes coming out to feed.

She searches for over an hour without success. By then she's thirsty. *One last try*, she thinks. And this time when she calls, someone answers. She gets such a fright she almost drops Nan's phone.

'Hello?' The voice is quiet and hesitant. Sounds like a kid, a boy.

'Who's that?' Tye asks.

No answer. She hears muffled breathing and crows in the background, probably the same ones that just flew past. 'Who's there? How did you get my phone?'

'Found it,' comes the sulky reply.

'Well, you have to give it back.'

'You reckon?' he says, 'I might, but—'

'But nothing. I want it back!'

There's a long silence, then Tye says, in a let's-be-reasonable voice, 'Look, I need my phone. You can't steal someone's property.'

'I didn't steal anything. Not before and not now!'

'All right, no need to yell. Where are you? Near the lake?'

No reply.

'Well, wherever you are I want my phone back. Tell me where you are and I'll come and get it.'

'No!'

'That's not fair. It doesn't belong to you.'

More silence. And then, cautiously, 'I could leave it somewhere for you.'

Tye thinks quickly. 'Do you know Chancy's Lodge?'

There's no answer but she hears twigs crackling underfoot and snuffly breathing. Whoever it is, he's walking somewhere, maybe walking away. Has she scared him off?

'Wait. Please. I really need my phone.'

The snuffly breathing stops and the boy is so still she can almost hear him thinking.

'You know that big stump where the track forks? I'll leave it there. But you have to give me something in return.'

Here it comes, she thinks. If this kid reckons she's going to pay for her own phone, he's got another think coming.

But it's not money the boy wants. 'I need some food.'

'What sort of food?'

'Anything. Bread and stuff. Cheese. Chocolate. And some apples and Weet-Bix, if you've got any. Oh, and a torch.'

'A torch? Why?'

'Listen, do you want your phone or don't you?'

'Course I do.'

'Then bring the stuff right now. Understand? And you mustn't tell anyone. Got that?'

'I can't bring it now. It'll be dark by the time I get home and come back.'

'Tomorrow then. First thing. If you don't come you'll never see your phone again.'

Just like blackmailers in crime movies. Tye almost laughs.

'I mean it,' the kid says. 'I'll chuck your phone in the lake.'

She doesn't doubt that he'll do it. That's something in his voice – something strung-out and reckless.

'What time?' she says. 'I need to—'

The screen goes blank. He's ended the call.

Tye puts Nan's phone away and picks up her bike. She's annoyed, but she wants her phone back, so she'd better do as he asks.

The sky's dark towards the end of the lake and she sees flickering in the distance. A storm, perhaps. If it rains tonight, at least her phone won't be lying in the open.

Five

The day is warm and muggy. Tye waves to Pop as she heads over to the house. He's talking to a couple of bushwalkers outside the visitors' accommodation block. They look a bit put out.

'It's up to you,' Pop's saying. 'But I'd strongly advise against it. The likelihood of dry lightning setting off fires in that area is pretty high.'

'You'd know, I guess,' one admits reluctantly.

'Might give it a miss and check out the museum at the old power station instead,' the other says.

'Wise choice,' Pop tells them.

Tye turns away. Through the open door of the office she spots Myrtle rootling in the overturned wastebasket. Nan will have a fit if she sees the mess.

'Now then, old girl,' Lance is saying, as he tries to scoop the contents up and replace them, 'steady on, we'll have Lena on our tail.'

Tye grins, helps him sort out the bin and ushers Myrtle outside.

In the kitchen, Nan's doing a million things at once, as usual, but she agrees that Tye may borrow her phone to search again for her own.

'Let me know the minute you find it,' Nan instructs. 'And don't wander too far. Pop's worried about the lightning strikes last night. He's bound to get a callout soon. Help yourself to leftover pie if you feel like it.'

Once Nan has bustled off to service the cabins, Tye peers into the fridge, puts the egg and bacon pie in a lunchbox, then adds a few slices of cheese, a chunk of salami and a large slice of cake. She can't find any Weet-Bix, but there's an unopened packet of muesli in the cupboard. It feels a bit sneaky, taking all this food behind Nan's back, but she shoves everything into a shopping bag. Adds a few apples from the fruit bowl, eating one as she goes.

Now what else did he want? Chocolate. There'll be chocolate biscuits in the store behind the office. She goes back to her cabin, grabs a pile of coins and leaves them on the office desk. That makes her feel a bit better. But she's cross. She doesn't want this boy complicating her life, but she does want her phone. She puts the bag in her bike basket and bumps off along the track.

Tye sees the lake through gaps between the trees. There's flickering over the hills on the far side of the water and the sky has turned a steely sort of grey. Very far away Tye can just make out a tiny thread of smoke.

When she reaches the stump there's nothing on it. *What a scammer!* Should she call the boy? She decides not to. Dumps the bag, turns around and rides away.

She doesn't go far, just out of sight. She quietly puts down the bike and ducks into the scrub at the side of the track, moving carefully so as not to make any sound.

When she gets near enough to see the bag, she settles behind a tree and waits. No sign of anyone. She pictures her phone sinking into the lake, along with all her contacts.

Then she sees a flash of yellow. Suddenly he's there – a scruffy boy in a dirty yellow cap, the same one she saw that day with Pop. Cropped hair, shorts and thongs. He's smaller than her, can't be more than eleven. He's carrying a daypack, wrong way round, so it hangs in front of him. He doesn't put the phone on the stump, just grabs the plastic bag and with a furtive look over his shoulder, slips back into the bush.

Tye's up and after him in a flash. 'Stop!' she yells. 'Hold it right there!'

Bushes slap her face and twigs scratch her arms as the yellow cap bobs ahead of her. Then the boy disappears. She can hear him crashing through the scrub, first heading one way and then another, like a startled animal.

She shoves her way after him, and when her T-shirt gets caught in the undergrowth she pulls free, tearing it. She's almost caught up to him when the scrub opens onto rocks and big clumps of cutting grass. The kid bounds ahead, dodging boulders. He's holding the backpack carefully so it doesn't bounce around. He looks behind, sees her gaining on him, then stumbles, dropping the shopping bag and plunging forward.

He breaks his fall with his hands. Tye could be on him in two seconds, but something holds her back. She stops and watches him pick himself up. He's out of breath. She is too. He leans against a rock, panting heavily, then slides to the ground and sits there cradling the pack in his arms and rocking. *He must be hurt*, she thinks, as she slowly approaches.

The boy stares at her fiercely. 'Look what you've done!'

He takes a deep breath before opening the backpack and anxiously peeping inside. He sighs with relief, then glares accusingly at Tye. 'I could have squashed her!'

Tye holds out her hand. 'Give me back my phone, then.'

The boy ignores her.

'Right now! That was the deal.'

His hand moves inside the pack. 'You're okay, little one,' he murmurs. He closes the backpack and sits catching his breath. 'That was close. If she got hurt it would've been your fault.'

Tye picks up the bag of food.

'Give it here,' the boy demands.

'Phone first,' she says.

The boy looks at her warily. 'How do I know what's in the bag? Might just be rubbish.'

Tye takes out an apple and throws it at him, hard. He catches it, bites off a piece and slips it into the backpack. Then he starts stuffing the rest into his mouth.

'Thanks,' he splutters, juice dripping down his chin.

Tye notices a small crescent-shaped scar on his temple. It moves in and out as he chews. He gulps down the apple, then takes out Tye's phone and places it on the ground. She snatches it up. When she hands over the bag he immediately begins digging into it. He pulls out the lunchbox, opens the lid and gasps.

'Egg and bacon – my favourite!' He looks up at Tye as if he's seeing her for the first time. She sits down on a tussock a short distance away.

The large chunk of pie is gone in a matter of seconds. Tye's never seen anyone gulp down food so fast. He takes out the cheese and salami and begins shoving everything into his mouth.

'Chocolate biscuits!' he cries, holding up the packet and spraying crumbs in her direction. 'Even better!'

Then he pulls out the box of muesli, shakes it and smiles. 'I'll save this for her.' He pats the backpack, and, slipping his arms out of the shoulder straps, places it carefully on the ground beside him.

'Thanks, Tye,' he says, taking another huge bite of bun.

Tye is taken aback. 'How do you know my name?'

'You get lots of messages.'

He takes out the piece of cake, examines it and puts it back in the bag, along with the biscuits.

'For later,' he says.

Tye looks the boy up and down. He's scrawny, his legs are scratched and badly sunburnt and the checked shirt he's wearing is dirty and much too big for him. And how he managed to run in thongs, she'll never know.

'Are you in trouble?' she asks.

His eyes narrow. 'What's it to you?'

Tye stands up. She's got her phone back. The exchange is complete.

When she turns to go the boy says, 'What about the torch?'

Tye shrugs. 'Forgot it.'

'I need a torch,' he insists. He gets to his feet and a shower of pie crumbs falls from his shirt.

'Well, there isn't one.' She stares at him and he stares back, then he drops his eyes.

'It would have been good to have a torch,' he says quietly.

'What's your name?' Tye asks.

The boy looks up in alarm. His face pales and the scar on his forehead stands out. 'Why? Did you hear something?'

'What do you mean?'

The kid looks at her for a long time as if he's weighing up whether or not to trust her with his name. 'Bailey,' he says finally.

'How old are you?' she asks.

'Fourteen.'

Tye raises her eyebrows. 'No way.'

'Well, *nearly* fourteen,' he says. 'I look young for my age.'

'More like twelve,' she says, 'if *that*.'

'All right, twelve, then. So what?'

'So you're by yourself and you have nothing to eat?'

'I'm waiting for me uncle. I don't need much, just some tucker to tide me over till he gets here. Can you get me some more? I'll pay you back.'

Tye looks at him doubtfully.

He puts on the backpack and gets up to leave. Tye follows him. Soon they're on a narrow path that climbs uphill. Now and then they get glimpses of the lake.

'Where are you going?' she calls after him.

The boy doesn't answer.

'Hey you, Bailey!' she shouts. 'What've you got in your pack?'

The boy stops and turns around. He pauses a moment, then folds back the top. Out pop two perky ears and a pointed face. 'Wallaby,' he says. 'She's mine. I call her Wanda.'

The joey's bigger than any of Carla's orphans.

'What happened to her mother?'

'Skittled.'

'Sad.'

'Yep. And the mongrel who did it didn't even stop. She was thrown out of her mum's pouch and I put her in mine.' He pats the top of the backpack. 'She probably still needs milk, but she can eat grass and fruit so she's doing all right.'

'How long have you had her?' Tye asks.

'Three days.'

'Where did you pick her up?'

Bailey closes the pack and looks intently at Tye. 'You're pretty nosy,' he says. 'Well, if you must know, up on Poatina Road near the pipeline.'

'That's a fair trek from here. What were you doing out there?'

He wipes his brow. 'Geez, it's getting warm. Did you see the light show last night?'

'I saw some flashes,' Tye replies.

'There were heaps.'

They reach the top of a rise and Tye can see the roof of Lakeview protruding from the trees. She can't see the road but hears a couple of cars go past.

The path ends at an embankment. Tall trees grow out of a tumble of boulders far below and there's a steep drop down to the water. Tye looks over the lake. It's hard to tell if that's smoke or clouds towards the south end of Broadwater. Smells like smoke.

'You been out there past the Neck?' Bailey asks, pointing.

Tye gazes at the narrow spit of land. The mud is crisscrossed with tyre tracks. Further out she can see the headland where she and Pop walked last year.

'Pity the lake's so low,' Bailey says, suddenly. 'Be a good place to hide out there when the Neck disappears.'

'Why would you want to hide?'

He gives her a sharp look. 'Yep, you're nosy all right.'

He finds a track that zigzags down to the water. 'Gotta go on me own from here,' he insists. 'You're not coming any further.'

Is this where he's been hiding? Tye thinks. But there's nothing here. Then she remembers Pop saying something about an old place somewhere nearby.

'You said you're waiting for your uncle. Where's he gone?' she asks.

'None of your business.' He puts his hand over his eyes and squints into the distance.

'So, what are you doing here on your own?'

He's immediately on the defence. 'Not my fault,' he says. 'It was that mongrel Carter. But the old fella'll sort it out when he comes back. Look at that!' He points to the sky.

A helicopter passes high overhead.

'That's a Firebird,' he cries. 'Single engine, I reckon.'

Tye notices the wind is picking up, a hot wind. She should be getting back. What's she doing out here with a runaway boy? Because she's pretty sure that's what Bailey is, and from the way he fired up when she mentioned stealing on the phone, she wouldn't be surprised if he's in trouble with the police.

'Who's Carter?' she asks.

But the boy doesn't answer. He wanders towards a patch of grass, and squats and opens the backpack. The wallaby leans out, rests her front paws on the ground and starts nibbling. After a few mouthfuls she hops right out and looks around.

Bailey takes off the backpack and sits on a rock. He gazes fondly at the wallaby.

'Awesome, isn't she?' he says.

'She's lovely,' Tye agrees.

'She doesn't run away, either. She knows I'm trying to help her.'

'Who's Carter?' Tye asks again. 'Did he persuade you to run away?'

'I didn't run away,' Bailey says. 'Anyway, me uncle'll sort it when he comes. He's not just me uncle, he's me *great*-uncle. And he *is* great, too.' A second helicopter comes into view on the far side of the lake. 'I'd love to fly one of them. You'd be able to see everything.'

A siren sounds in the distance.

Something doesn't add up. There's a lot the boy isn't telling. Bailey picks up the backpack. 'Watch this,' he says, holding it low so it gapes open. 'Hey Wanda, hop in.'

The wallaby bounds towards him and leaps in head-first, doing a somersault.

Tye can't help laughing. 'Little acrobat!'

Bailey laughs too. Then his shoulders start to heave and his fists clench. Tye steps back, not sure what's coming next. Surely he's not going to burst into tears.

Six

Bailey's bottom lip's quivering. Tye doesn't know what to do. She puts a tentative hand on his sleeve but he flinches away.

'Auntie Bev won't know where I am,' he spits out. 'She'll think I've done a runner. She trusted me. I was her favourite.'

Then a phone sounds, Nan's phone. *She's probably calling from the office phone to find out where I am.* But it's not Nan, it's Pop. He's in a hurry.

'Hi Tye, put your grandmother on, would you.'

'She's not here, Pop. I've borrowed her phone.'

'Well, tell her I won't be back for a while with the way things are looking.'

A siren starts up in the background. It's loud and he shouts over it. 'Have to go. See you, chicken.'

'Okay, I'll tell her,' Tye says and turns back to Bailey who's standing like a statue, staring at nothing. She picks up the shopping bag and pulls out the packet of chocolate biscuits. 'Here,' she says, shoving it in his direction.

'These might help. They're probably a bit melted by now though.'

Bailey drops his head as he takes a biscuit.

'She'll worry,' he says. 'She'll think I've cleared out.'

'Your Auntie Bev?'

He starts to speak and a bit of biscuit goes down the wrong way. He coughs and chokes. His eyes stream and he almost throws up. Should she whack him on the back? The chunk of biscuit flies out, along with a stream of saliva. Tye waits for him to catch his breath. She's finding it hard to follow his story. Stick with the facts, she tells herself.

'How did you get here – to the Neck, I mean?' she asks, looking across the water.

'Walked to Craig's Bay. Got over to this side in a tinny. Had a hard time getting the outboard going, but I can handle a boat. Been fishing with me uncle plenty of times. Anyway, I gotta go.' He turns away. 'Be seeing you,' he says, but he doesn't move.

Tye looks at him with concern. It takes her a while to realise he's waiting for her to leave first. When she turns to go, he holds out his hand. 'It was good to meet you, Tye. I didn't have anyone to talk to before you came, except Wanda.'

She shakes his hand, thinking there's something old-fashioned about him. He's like a little old man.

'You won't say nothing, will you?'

'All right,' she says.

'Promise?'

She nods.

He sighs with relief. 'Thanks a million.' Suddenly he looks worn out.

Tye hesitates. There's a lot she still doesn't understand. Maybe she ought to tell an adult – Nan or Pop, perhaps – and let them figure out what to do about Bailey. Perhaps she could ask Lily what she thinks. It wouldn't be dobbing on Bailey, really, and Lily is always full of ideas. Yep, that's what she'll do, she'll talk to Lily. This is too much to handle on her own.

'I'll see you then.' She turns to go.

'Wait,' he says. 'You can come with me, if you like. You'd probably find out anyway, a nosy person like you.'

So Tye follows Bailey along the shore. He carries the backpack over his shoulder and Wanda's head nods in time with his steps. As they leave the lake and head up a grassy path Tye notices a dinghy, half hidden in the bushes. It's shiny and new.

The path leads into some trees. 'There,' he says, pointing. 'Me uncle built it. I've stayed here plenty of times.'

The shack's hard to see because it blends so perfectly with the surrounding scrub. It's an old vertical board place, its palings dry and silver with age. A makeshift step leads to a veranda. There's a lean-to on one side, two posts and a rusty roof. A sheet of iron has come loose and is banging in the wind. The car parked underneath looks as if it hasn't been used for a while – it has flat tyres and a windscreen splattered with bird mess from a nest above.

Bailey puts the bag of food on the veranda and plonks down beside it. He holds the backpack on his lap. 'The place is a bit messy inside. Auntie Bev would go berserk. I'll help clean it up when the old bloke comes back.'

'Bailey, is your uncle's name Reg?'

'You know him?'

Tye shakes her head and mumbles, 'No. Just heard of him.'

She peers through the window rather than look at Bailey. The shack's a rat heap – rubbish in the fireplace, shredded magazines on the floor, a nest of moth-eaten blankets at one end of an ancient couch, a pile of old clothes at the other.

'Bailey, you can't stay here.'

Then her phone sounds. This time it's Nan.

'You found the phone then?'

'Yeah, thanks Nan. It was just beside the—'

'Listen, love, come home right now, would you? Where are you?'

'Um, just along the track.'

'I need to go and open up the hall. Just a minute—'

Tye hears voices in the background. When Nan comes back she sounds distracted. 'Things are changing fast. It's those strikes, Tye. They've started fires all over the place. Be quick, can you?'

Nan ends the call.

As soon as Tye puts down her phone, Nan's phone sounds. The caller speaks before she has time to say hello.

'Lena, it's Joan from over at Atholmere. How are things looking up your way? There's a lot of smoke here, probably from spot fires, but I heard there's a big blaze out of the back of Little Pine Lagoon, less than ten kays west of Merrick. Do you know—'

'It's not Lena,' Tye interrupts. 'It's her granddaughter.'

'Sorry, love. Is your nan there?'

'No. I think she's going to the hall.'

'Right. I'll ring her there. Stay safe.' The lady hangs up.

Stay safe? What's that supposed to mean? There's no fire around here.

'I have to go home,' Tye tells Bailey. 'Why don't you come with me?'

Bailey's eyes grow wide. 'Don't you understand, Tye? I'm in big trouble.'

'But you've done nothing wrong.' Tye looks back towards the dinghy and wonders if this is true. 'My grandparents might be able to help sort things out.'

Bailey shakes his head and reaches into his pocket, pulling out a key. He unlocks the door and goes into the one-room shack. Tye follows him inside. Last year's calendar hangs on the wall, open at July. Flanking it are fishing photos and a series of kids' drawings.

'I did them.'

'They're good. How old were you?'

'Seven maybe. Not bad for a little tyke, eh?'

He points. 'That's me best one. It's a fort me uncle told me about down near Bronte Park. He helped build it. A sort of castle, half underground. It's called a bunker.'

Then he catches Tye looking about her. 'Possums have been in,' he says. 'Guess they came down the chimney. Big mess, eh?'

Not just the shack, Tye thinks, *the whole situation*. She's trying to get her head around it.

'Look, Bailey. You can't stay here on your own.'

Bailey takes a deep breath. 'Just bring me a bit more food and a torch.'

Reluctantly, Tye agrees. 'If I can. I'll come tomorrow. But right now I need to go home. You're sure you won't come?'

Bailey doesn't answer.

She looks over her shoulder. There's thick bush growing right up to the side of the shack.

'If a fire came through you'd have no chance,' she says.

'You think I'm an idiot? I'd go down to the lake.' Bailey grabs her arm, and his grip is surprisingly strong. 'I can't come. You gotta realise that. And you mustn't tell anyone. You won't, will you?' He stares at her with fear in his eyes.

'Please,' he begs. 'Promise me.'

'I already promised,' she says.

'Thanks, Tye. Thanks heaps.'

Tye's phone sounds again but she ignores it. Bailey points to an overgrown track behind the shack.

'When it forks, go left,' he tells her.

She heads off, walking fast. She thought she was close to the Lakeview turnoff, but it takes a while to reach it. By now the day is sweltering. Tye wonders what time it is but doesn't check. She breaks into a run and is glad when she sees the stump and the old blue bike waiting in the bushes.

Tye feels as if she's been far away, almost to another country. She throws her leg over the saddle and heads for home, pedalling fast. Nan's phone sounds several times but she doesn't stop to answer it.

When she next catches sight of the lake it's taken on a strange coppery sheen. There's a vast plume of smoke in the west. What did that woman say? A big blaze behind Little Pine Lagoon? The conservation area starts near there and behind it is the national park where all the pencil pines grow. Tye hopes it's not heading in that direction.

She's almost at Chancy's when she sees Lance on the track. He holds up his hand like a policeman. As she stops beside him, he puts a finger to his lips.

'A word of warning,' he whispers. 'Someone's in strife.'

'What do you mean, Lance?' she pants.

'Could be Myrtle. Or it could be me. Or it could be you, Opal. Lena's not happy.'

'I'm not Opal, remember? I'm Tyenna.'

'Of course you are. What's the matter with me? My apologies, young lady.'

Tye fishes Nan's phone out of her pocket and hurries up the path between the cabins. Nan is carrying a pile of blankets to the car. She dumps them in the back and turns to Tye, hands on hips and mouth set in a grim line.

'Where on earth have you been? Well?'

'I'm sorry, Nan. I . . . the phone . . . sorry it took so long.' Already Tye's regretting her promise to Bailey.

Nan shakes her head in disbelief. 'Have you got any idea what's been going on? There are fires all over the place. Your grandfather hasn't stopped since first thing this morning. Didn't I ask you to hurry back?'

Nan's phone rings again and Tye hands it over.

'Yes, Aileen. I'm bringing them. I'll be right there.'

She turns back to Tye. 'I was beginning to think I should call Brendan, but the police are the last people you'd want to trouble at a time like this. They're flat out. Everyone is.'

'Sorry, Nan. I really am. I didn't know.'

Nan gives her a quick hug. 'I'm just glad you're back,' she says. 'Would you mind looking after things here for me, please?'

'Of course.'

Nan is getting into the car. 'Don't take any bookings. Thanks, love.' She squeezes Tye's hand. 'Sorry about the outburst. We're all a bit stressed.'

As Nan drives away, Tye gazes after her in shock.

Several guests check out; some are walkers, others tourists.

'We're leaving now in case the roads close,' one woman tells her.

Tye goes to the kitchen. How long is it since breakfast? Feels like ages. She downs several glasses of water, helps herself to some lunch, then sits at the table and checks her messages.

Heaps from Lily from early the day before. One from Opal. Shoot's tomorrow. Wish me luck. The job, always the job. A message from Lukas who tells her that the climate rally date is confirmed. Whoohoo, he says, We're away! And he's onto a new project for the science club even though it's holidays. Time – eons, epochs, eras, all the periods. It's epic, Tye. There are more recent messages from Lil. Did you find it or not? Guess not.

I found more than the phone, Tye thinks.

Pop's late getting home. Tye's in bed when she hears the ute pull into the drive. She gets up, puts on her hoodie and goes to the kitchen. Her grandparents are talking about the day's events.

'That tree that caught fire on the wind farm was just the start,' Pop's saying. 'They'd put it out by the time we arrived but even on the way there we saw lighting flashing along the ridgeline. Bolts were hitting nearly every peak.' He wipes his brow, his face stained with soot and sweat. 'And as soon as we headed back we started getting more calls. There were spot fires wherever the bands of lightning had passed. We went all over the place. Seven fires in one day.'

He goes off to have a shower, comes back in pyjamas and joins them at the table.

'The big fire's going behind the Great Pine Tier. Parks and Wildlife Service are looking after that. They're putting in containment lines, trying to stop it getting into the Walls. Glad I turned those walkers around when I did.'

'The carpark behind Merrick Hotel was chockers,' Nan says. 'Help arriving from all over.'

'More tankers coming tomorrow,' Pop tells her. 'We'll need to offer some beds.'

'Aileen's onto it. We've opened the hall. Where did you finish up?'

'East of Little Pine Lagoon. After we went down to London Lakes.'

Nan gets up to put on the kettle. Pop turns to Tye and gives her a weary smile. 'How was your day, chicken?' he asks.

Tye doesn't know what to say. There's nothing she *can* say. Why did she ever make that stupid pact with the boy.

'Heard you copped a bit of flak from Nan here,' Pop says, with a nod towards Nan's back.

'I lost track of time,' she says.

'Yes, but best to stay close when there are fires about.' He yawns, leaning back in his chair. He looks done in. 'I'm ready to hit the sack.'

Tye says goodnight and heads back to her cabin. She was tired before, but now she's full of restless energy. She sits on her bed, phone in hand, and does some searching. Finds a lightning map. Over two thousand strikes in thirty hours. How many of these started fires? And how many of the fires are burning through the night?

She thinks of Bailey, alone in the crummy old shack. As far as she can see the fires are nowhere near there. Nowhere near Chancy's, either – but she has to admit this summer is not turning out to be as much fun as she expected.

She picks up the phone. It's time to tell Lily.

Seven

Tye wakes to a call from Opal.

'What's wrong, Mum?'

'Does something have to be wrong for a mother to ring her daughter?'

'I guess not.' Tye sits up and rubs her eyes. She hasn't slept well. 'It's just early for you, that's all.' She yawns. Usually Opal's not up until mid-morning.

'How are things, hon?' Opal asks.

'All right.' Tye says, trying to keep her voice normal. 'But it would have been great if you'd called on my birthday.'

'Oh my gosh! I forgot! How could I? What sort of mother am I? Forgetting her child's birthday. What an airhead!'

Tye feels even more exhausted. She's not in the mood for her mother's dramatics.

She opens the blind. The sky's still smoky but the water looks normal, a bluey-grey colour, not the harsh bronze it was yesterday.

'Tye, I've got some good news.'

There's scratching at the door. 'Hold on a minute, Mum.'

When she opens the door Myrtle barges in. Someone must have had the outside tap on, because her paws are muddy.

'No, Myrtle. No!' Tye yells, suddenly wide awake. In a few seconds her clean floor is a mess of muddy pawprints.

'Don't tell me Myrtle's still around?' Opal says.

'Yes, still here. What were you saying, Mum?'

'I did well yesterday. I'm under consideration. I'll have to go in a sec. They're setting up now for an early morning test shoot.'

'That's good,' Tye says, nudging Myrtle out the door. Pop is getting into the ute, his overalls covered in yesterday's soot and grime. He's scoffing down a piece of toast. Must have been called out again.

'How's everything there?' Opal asks. 'Mum and Dad all right?'

'Yep. They're fine.'

'Uh-oh. There's my call. Got to run, babe!'

As usual, it's all about Opal. But at least she called.

Tye looks at the time. Seven-thirty. Time to get moving. She's arranged to meet Lily at eight. Lil was agog at the news last night.

Tye slips into the guests' kitchen. She finds a big plastic bag and helps herself to some of the stuff left behind: cheese, a box of crunchy granola – Wanda will appreciate that – three slightly bruised pears, and a couple of cans of baked beans. Although there's a sign on the cupboard in her grandmother's neat printing – *PLEASE USE* – she's starting to feel like a burglar. She puts the bag of food in her cabin and goes to the house for breakfast.

'I worry about your pop,' Nan says, running her fingers through her hair. 'It's hard work fighting fires and he's not as young as he used to be.' The laptop's open on the table. Nan peers at the screen.

'It's bad down the Huon,' she says, 'and just look at the South West.' She points to the map. Pencil pine zone, Tye notices.

Her grandmother turns on the radio. *The area is now over twenty thousand hectares and the fact that the fires are burning in peat means they may continue for weeks to come, even months. Sprinkler lines are protecting sensitive alpine communities . . .*

'I guess you'll be wanting to spend the day with Lily, as usual.'

Tye nods.

'Could you ask her to come over here? I'll feel more comfortable if you're not wandering about in the bush. I have to get down to the hall. Aileen's there already with a couple of volunteers. They're making food packs for the RATs.'

'Yuck,' says Tye. 'Why are you feeding rats?'

Nan chuckles. 'Not actual rats, love. The Remote Area Team. We call them the RATs.'

When Nan leaves the kitchen Tye has a look in the drawer, finds a spare torch and slips it in her shoulder bag. Bailey could do with a decent blanket, too. The nights can be cold even in the middle of summer – it's been known to snow in January. The blankets in the shack are filthy and threadbare. Bailey'd be cold at night. Lonely and scared as well.

She goes into the linen store. Suddenly the door opens and Nan appears, carrying a stack of sheets. Her eyebrows rise in surprise.

'I was just . . . I can do the cabins if you like, Nan,' Tye says.

'Thanks, love. There's just the three – Lakeside, Rainbow and Snowgum. I'd really appreciate it. I've got to get back to Merrick. You'll be okay here with Lance?'

Tye nods. 'There's something Lil and I have to do first, but I'll be quick.'

'Straight there and straight back, all right? I need to know where you are, in case we have to move fast.'

Tye nods again, not quite meeting Nan's eye.

'Good girl. I know I can count on you.'

Tye texts Lily – Running late wait for me – then rushes through the chores and goes to pick up the bag. She looks at her brand-new sleeping bag and is ashamed of her hesitation. What's she worried about? That he'll steal it? Make it dirty? Nan's got an old one in the hall cupboard. She'll give him that. She puts it in the plastic bag and pedals off.

Bailey ought to call his Auntie Bev, she thinks, as she rides to Lil's. *I have to try to persuade him.*

It's after nine when she arrives at Lakeview, but Lily's butterfly curtains are still drawn. Her dad is outside, checking over an enormous truck parked in the drive.

'Hello, Tye,' Brett says. 'Gonna be a hot one, eh. I'm due at work today but I'm thinking I might stay home.'

'Because of the fires?'

'Reckon,' he says, rubbing his chin. 'They're nowhere near us, but you never know.'

He goes up onto the deck and raps on Lily's window. 'Rise and shine, Sunshine. Tye's here.'

Tye slips her bag underneath the stairs to save any questions.

'Sleeps like a log, that girl,' Brett says.

Carla opens the sliding door. 'Morning, Tye. I know I say it every time, but . . . surprise, surprise . . . you're just in time for the feeds!'

Tye nods. 'Have to be quick, though. Lil and I have plans. And Nan wants me back home soon.'

'Okay,' Carla says, and turns to Lil's dad. 'Still here, Brett? Having second thoughts about going in?'

'Yep. Give us a look at that list again.'

'We've pretty much done it all – leaves, gutters, vegetation.'

Lily appears at the door, yawning. Bed hair and rumpled pyjamas. She grabs Tye's hand and pulls her inside. 'Sorry. Slept in. But I'll be ready in ten for our rescue mission.' Her eyes sparkle. 'Oh, but there's the feeds to do first.'

Tye swallows down her misgivings and tries not to betray her impatience as she works through the tasks. There's one full bottle of formula left over and she slips it into her shoulder bag. They hear Brett's truck rumbling away down the drive.

'He must have decided it's safe to leave,' Lily says.

Carla glances at the checklist. 'I wonder if he boarded up the crawl space.' She goes outside and peers under the deck. Pulls out the big plastic bag. 'What's this, Lil?'

'It's mine,' Tye says. 'It's got food in it, so I put it in the shade.'

Carla's phone rings then and she springs back inside to answer it.

Lily checks the bag's contents. 'I've got a stash as well, for our *fugitive*. Should keep him going for a bit.'

Carla reappears, phone to her ear. 'Thanks, Lena. I'll go straight over. Tye? She's right here . . . Okay, see you soon.'

Carla turns to the girls. 'Someone's left a joey at Chancy's. Would have dropped it in here but he was going the other way. I'll be straight back. Tye, your nan says to remind you not to be too long.'

The girls ride north along the main road. A short way past the turn-off to Barry's, they spot a track sloping towards the lake.

'Down here,' Lily says. She knows these tracks well. They head down to the shack.

Tye worries how Bailey will react when he sees Lily. 'You know that chart you gave me for my birthday, Lil?' she says. 'It said I had an important pledge to keep. Do you think I've broken that pledge by telling someone else about Bailey?'

'Not just *someone*,' Lily mock-protests, 'your best friend. You know you can trust me.'

There's no sign of Bailey at the shack. They look in the window. The blankets are in the same heap at the end of the couch. Looks like he hasn't slept in them. The only indication that he's been there is the empty chocolate biscuit packet lying on the table.

Tye tries the door. It opens. She puts the plastic bag inside and is turning to leave when Bailey appears through the trees, Wanda hopping along beside him. Tye can't help noticing how haggard he appears. It's not just the ragged clothes; he has a hunched look, as if he's shrivelling.

'Saw you coming,' he says. 'I was watching.' He narrows his eyes and points to Lily. 'Who's she? Why'd you bring her here? You said you wouldn't dob on me, Tye.'

'I didn't,' Tye replies. 'Chill.'

Lily extends her hand. 'You're safe with me, boyo.'

Bailey shoves his hands into his pockets and looks away.

'Where did you sleep?' Tye asks.

'Over there.' He waves vaguely behind him. 'Too risky to sleep in the shack.'

'Risky? Why?'

'First place they'd look.'

They go into the shack. Bailey opens the bag and begins rummaging through it. Lily places her bag close by. When Tye holds out the feeding bottle to him his face shines with gratitude. 'Oh wow. Thanks. Just what she needs.'

'Hey,' Lily says, 'did you ask Mum if you could take that?'

Tye blushes and Bailey keeps a firm hold on the bottle. Wanda seems puzzled at first but the milk is still warm and once she gets the scent she starts tugging away at the teat.

'Where'd you get it?' he asks.

'Lily's mum's a wildlife carer.'

He stares at her in alarm. 'You tell her?'

'Course not. I promised, didn't I?'

Bailey takes out the sleeping bag. 'Gee, thanks, Tye. It gets pretty cold at night.'

He digs into the food bag. 'Baked beans. Great.' He finds the torch and slips it into his pocket. 'Thanks.'

'Bailey,' Tye interrupts. 'We think you should call your Auntie Bev.'

He bites his lip and frowns.

Tye holds out the phone. 'Call her and tell her you're all right. She'll be worried about you.'

'Can't,' he says. 'Not now.' But he's looking at the phone and Tye knows he's wavering.

'Just do it.'

Bailey stares at the phone for a long time before he reaches for it. He slowly thumbs in Auntie Bev's number. Lifts the phone to his ear. 'It's me,' he says quietly after a moment.

Tye can't hear the reply, but it's obviously not what Bailey was expecting. He looks baffled. Stutters a bit. 'Yeah . . . no . . . yeah . . . cool . . . you know, swimming and stuff . . . will do . . . say hi to the others . . . Was Benny alright? . . . just an earache . . . yeah . . . okay . . . bye, Auntie Bev.'

He hands back the phone and looks into space. 'She thinks I'm at camp,' he mutters. 'She didn't say anything about the car. Carter must have got it back without her finding out. She said thanks for calling her, for being so thoughtful.'

'What car?' Lily says.

'Is that where you're supposed to be, at camp?' Tye asks.

He nods.

'So how come the camp people didn't tell her you never arrived?'

Bailey shrugs. 'Carter, I reckon. He'd spin some story. Probably told her I'd gone off to camp, and then told the camp people I wasn't coming. Yeah, that'd be it. He's pretty tricky, that one. And no good telling on him. He makes sure you regret it.'

'Why didn't you tell her where you really are?'

Bailey looks down. 'She might send me away.'

'Your auntie wouldn't do that!' Tye says.

'Well, you see . . .' Bailey's voice is low and hesitant. 'She's not really my auntie, she's a carer.'

Tye's head is spinning. 'So, you and Carter aren't related?'

Bailey shakes his head.

'Well, that's one thing you can be glad of, anyway.'

Bailey gives a weak grin.

'Your life sure is full of complications,' Lil says. 'I don't know how you're ever going to sort things out.'

'But maybe we can help you,' Tye tells him.

'Time to spill the whole story, brother,' Lil says. 'For starters' – she points to the scar on Bailey's temple – 'how'd you get that?'

Bailey doesn't seem to resent Lily's direct question. 'Same place I got these.' He shows the inside of his arms. There are burn marks on his wrists. 'Carter's work.'

'Sounds like a head case.'

'He is. And I had to share a room with him.'

'So he's behind whatever mess you've got yourself into, I'm guessing.'

Bailey nods.

'Spill it,' Lily encourages. 'If we're to help you sort this out we need the facts.'

'Well, I live in a group home,' Bailey says. 'Me and these other kids. It was good till Carter came. Then a few days ago, I was telling them about the massive bunker, that me uncle helped to build.'

'The one in your drawing?' Tye says.

'Yep. I didn't even know Carter was listening. He said I had to show him where it was.'

'You could've said no,' Lil tells him.

'To Carter? You're joking. Anyway, he sneaked Auntie Bev's car keys.' Bailey turns to the girls, wide-eyed. 'I never knew Carter could drive!'

'What? Stealing cars!' It's worse than Tye imagined.

'Not me. It was Carter,' Bailey insists, and sighs. 'When they realised I didn't know the way, they dumped me out and chucked a U-ey. That's when Wanda's mum got killed, and I borrowed the dinghy and came over here.'

He scowls ferociously, and rubs his eyes. 'Blasted wind. Dust everywhere.' His burns are livid arcs on his grubby arms. 'And now the cops'll be after me. They'll put me in Barton Hall with the really bad kids. That's where Carter was, before.'

Lily whistles. 'Seriously bad news, that place. You want to stay out of it at all costs.'

Tye looks at Bailey's damaged wrists and her stomach churns. Poor kid. No parents *and* having to put up with being bullied. No wonder he's a mess. Her own mum might seem a bit flaky, but with Jas as her rock, and Nan and Pop loving her to bits, she's pretty lucky, all told. What does she know of Barton Hall and what might or might not happen to Bailey there? The place is probably full of Carters.

'Well, we're on your case now,' Lil says. 'You can relax.'

Tye hopes Lily has a plan up her sleeve.

Bailey's slumping with relief, looking from one girl to the other, his eyes brimming. 'Dunno how to thank you . . .'

'We have to leave you for a bit, now,' Lily says to Bailey. 'Will you be okay?'

'I need to get back to Nan's,' Tye adds. 'I got into trouble yesterday.' *Though my trouble is nothing compared with Bailey's*, she thinks.

He nods, sniffing. 'And thanks for the stuff, Tye, Lily.'

'Mega adventure!' Lil says as they collect their bikes.

For us, maybe but not so much for Bailey. But she's glad she doesn't have to carry his secret on her own.

Eight

'**This is big,** Lil says,' as they push their bikes towards the road. 'We need a plan. I think we should start with a bath.'

Tye gives Lil a sideways look. What's she thinking? The boy needs more than a bath!

'First things first, as Mum used to say during her community nursing days,' Lil continues. 'When there's so many problems to tackle, you start with the basics. Get the patient clean and fed. Then work out what's next.'

Tye looks at her friend doubtfully. Her phone sounds. Probably Nan. 'We'll talk about it later, Lil, I've got to get home now. Come over as soon as you can.'

Tye throws her leg over the bike and waves goodbye.

'I'll make a list,' Lil yells as Tye rides away.

By the time Tye gets back, the wind has picked up and she hears the wailing of sirens. Dirt and leaves from the newly cleared area are swirling around the carpark. The heat is intense. Lance is on the phone in the office.

'What name did you say the booking was in?' He runs a gnarled finger down Nan's list on the desk in front of him, ignoring the Post-it note beside it: *Lance, no bookings this week. Thanks, Lena.*

'Ah, Fulmore, yes. Now what was the problem?'

Lance touches his hat and gives Tye a wink, then frowns with concentration.

'But why wouldn't it be safe, Mrs Fulmore? Just a minute.' He puts down the phone and sighs. 'I don't know what she's talking about.' He looks out the window. The remaining guests are packing up, putting fishing rods on top of their car. 'Excuse me a moment.'

Lance gets halfway across the yard then stops and looks back, holding his hat against the wind. 'Tyenna,' he yells, 'would you be so kind as to deal with that call?'

Tye takes a message and puts down the phone. Then she goes after Lance. Nan's going to be really mad if he's taken any bookings.

Lance is at the car, shaking hands with the two men who are leaving.

'It's been an honour to meet you,' one of them shouts, holding up his arm to shield his face from the dust. 'My dad's not going to believe it when I tell him I've been fishing with the legendary Lance Armitage.'

'I'm only sorry I didn't get to show you my best spots. Anyway, you did all right.' Lance nods towards the esky in the back of the car.

The second fellow brings out a camera. 'I wonder if you'd mind?'

'Not at all. If you like, I'll get my trophies.'

Lance walks briskly towards his room, so Tye leaves him to it. No point in telling him about the bookings. He'll forget as soon as she's spoken. Is this memory thing serious? she wonders. Mistaking her for her mother, muddling up the bookings. But he's old. And old people do forget things.

She goes to the kitchen. Nan has left the radio on. *Firefighters forced to trek for two hours through rugged terrain to reach a fire front.* At least Pop isn't doing that, she tells herself as she checks her phone.

A text from Lukas. Thinking about deep time.

She sends him a row of question marks.

Like zillions of years ago, he replies, before the Anthropocene.

There's a text from Lily: List nearly complete – see you soon.

Good. Tye's glad Lily's on board.

The radio drones on. *High fire danger throughout the state. Fifty bushwalkers airlifted to safety.* Tye's only half listening. She's thinking about Bailey. And his uncle. The shack's pretty derelict. No power, and no running water. So much for Lily's bath idea.

Lance comes to the door, having farewelled the guests. He looks windblown and excited. He's always pleased to get his trophies out.

'What was the problem with that booking?' he asks.

'No problem, Lance. I took a message. Nan'll fix it when she comes home.'

Lance notices the laptop on the kitchen table and peers at the map on the screen. Little triangle-shaped icons are scattered across Tasmania, some yellow, some orange and some red. 'What's all this then?'

'Fire warnings,' Tye says vaguely. 'Lance, do you know someone called Reg Stokes?'

'Rings a bell but not a loud one.'

A car pulls up in the carpark and Lance looks up. 'The guests,' he says, heading out the door. 'Maybe they forgot something.'

But it's not the guests, it's Carla. Lily climbs out of the car and Carla drives away.

'Crazy weather. Hot as,' Lil says. 'Wind nearly blew us off the road. Mum's off to Merrick. She'll pick me up on the way back. We haven't got long.'

They go to Tye's cabin and with the door firmly closed behind them, Lily unfolds a large sheet of paper. It's a confusion of swirly lines and arrows.

'I've been brainstorming,' she says, 'but it's no good. Even if we provide the basics he can't stay by himself much longer.' She's looking less confident now.

'He's not by himself,' Tye says. 'He's got us. And he won't be there forever, just till his uncle Reg comes.'

Lily looks at her, wide-eyed. 'Reg? What's his other name?'

'Stokes, I think.'

Lily gives a deep sigh. 'I should have expected this. We're heading into a total lunar eclipse and Saturn is squaring Uranus. That means anything can happen.' She sighs again. 'His uncle won't be coming. That old man died months ago. Well, maybe it was longer. I'm not sure. He went into a nursing home in Longford, I think.

Mum and Dad knew him. Nice old fellow. Friendly to everyone. Even friends with Barry. Those two were mates, you know.'

'Poor Bailey. Maybe we can't sort this out, Lil. We might need to contact his Auntie Bev, or get him to call her again.'

'And risk him ending up in Barton Hall?' Lily says. 'But maybe Barry could help.'

'The Hermit of Hutt's Hill?'

'Old Reg and Barry worked together for years, ages ago, building sheds and stuff. Barry might be prepared to help his mate's great-nephew.'

Tye thinks of the dogs and gulps. Then a car horn sounds.

'That's Mum.' Lil takes Tye's hand and squeezes it. 'We'll work this out somehow. You and me together, like we told him.'

Tye goes back to the kitchen. She looks at the laptop. Most of the fires are down south but there are a few in the Highlands. She clicks a triangle west of Merrick and reads the information: *Warning level – Advice – Stay Informed, Status – Going, Size – 55 hectares.* The bush animals – will they have time to get out? Which reminds her of Myrtle. Hopefully she's in Lance's room. Better make sure.

Nan rings. 'Everything all right, Tye?' Sounds like she's in a vehicle.

'Yep, all good.' *Checking up on me*, Tye thinks.

'I'm on my way back from Launceston right now, with a van full of supplies for the community hall, including an extra fridge and a generator. Keep tomorrow free, love. We're going to need all the help we can get.'

Nan says she's almost at Merrick. 'I shouldn't be late home, Tye, but who knows what might happen. See you soon, hopefully.'

When Tye knocks on Lance's door, there's no answer so she looks inside. His tools are lined up on the table but there's no sign of him or Myrtle. He's the one who should be looking after the wombat. Where is he?

She checks the laundry and bathrooms but Lance isn't there. He's not in the guests' kitchen or common room either. Then she checks the office. No Lance, but Myrtle's been there. She's knocked over Nan's small filing cabinet. Its contents are strewn across the floor. Tye doesn't stop to pick them up.

She searches the house and cabins, even her own. Looks in the shed where the lifejackets and paddles are kept. Lance is nowhere to be found. Could he have gone fishing? Not likely. Not in this weather. It's too hot to be outside. She considers calling Nan.

Tye hears another siren passing. Sees helicopters rising from the Merrick end of the lake. She goes down to the water and there's Lance wading through the shallows, his trousers rolled up above his skinny shanks. He's wearing a giant pair of Polaroids and he's lost his hat. His rod is on the shore.

'Lance, what are you doing?' she calls.

He mumbles something and stumbles towards her. The wind is almost strong enough to blow him over.

Tye puts her hand under his elbow. 'You shouldn't be out in this wild weather.'

'Nonsense, girlie. It blows the cobwebs away,' Lance says, but he looks a bit wonky and once she gets him back to his room he drinks three glasses of water straight off and then lies down with a groan.

Tye is still putting the office to rights when Nan arrives home.

'What's happened here?' she asks, although it's obvious. 'To tell you the truth, Tye, I could do without this right now. Your pop and I are going to have to sort something out about Lance. Things can't go on like this. And I don't just mean letting Myrtle run riot. It's getting to the point where—'

'He wandered off,' Tye interrupts. 'I was going to call you.'

'Not your problem, Tye,' Nan says. 'Now just leave the rest of those papers. I'll sort them later.' A small plane roars overhead and Nan steps outside to watch it pass. 'The first of the Air Tractors,' she says. 'Kevin said they were coming. They're going to be a big help. Their belly tanks hold three thousand litres.'

'Kevin?'

'He's in charge at the hall.'

'I thought you were in charge, you and Aileen.'

'He's coordinating the fire effort. The office there is his control centre. Wall-to-wall computers, maps and pinboards.' She gives a weary sigh. 'How about making your nan a cuppa? Let's hope Pop's not late tonight.'

Tye thinks of her pop and then thinks of Bailey. Pop would know how to help. She wishes she could ask him. But she's given Bailey her word.

The wind doesn't let up and the day doesn't cool down until after they have eaten. When it gets dark Tye can see flashing lights on the road. Pop isn't late home, but that doesn't mean the fires are any better, he tells Tye. If anything, they're worse.

Tye waters her pencil pine and goes to bed early. But she can't sleep. It's well after midnight when she notices lights on in the house. She gets up and goes along the walkway. Nan and Pop are sitting at the kitchen table, listening to the fire report on the radio. The laptop is open on the weather page: the seven-day forecast for Merrick.

'We could be in for the long haul with this,' Pop says. 'Or it might all be over in the next couple of days.'

Tye looks at the screen – zero chance of rain, steadily increasing temperatures, high winds.

She sits with her grandparents for a while. When she goes back to bed she finds herself looking up the lightning map again. The strikes are over for the time being, but the damage is done. *Well, not done but begun,* she thinks. And her mind returns to Bailey. They need to tell him about his uncle. His *great*-uncle. He needs to know. She'll do it first thing tomorrow.

Nine

Nan pokes her head in the cabin door early the next morning. 'Tye, I want you and Lance to come with me to the hall today,' she says. 'Things have stepped up. It's all hands to the pump and I don't want to be worrying about Lance while I'm flat out at the hall.' She's gone before Tye is properly awake. *So there* is *a problem,* Tye thinks.

She hears a crash. Goes outside to look. The Lodge signboard is lying on the ground and a wheelie bin has emptied itself into the car park. Cans are rolling about.

'Help me pick those cans up, would you, Tye,' Nan shouts into the wind. 'We'll put the wheelie bins in the shed.'

In no time they're on their way south. It's mail run day, but with Pop out fighting fires and Nan needed at the hall, the mail will have to wait.

'Myrtle can fend for herself for the day,' Nan says as she pulls up. 'Just hope she stays out of trouble.'

People are milling about outside the hall and the carpark is overflowing. Aileen comes hurrying out.

'Good, you're here, Lena,' she says. 'Morning, Tye, Lance.'

'Whose are all these cars?' Tye asks.

'Locals, fire crew, visiting firefighters,' Aileen replies. 'And a heap of volunteers. We need every bit of help we can get.'

Inside, Tye stares at all the maps on the walls.

'The latest were brought in by helicopter early this morning,' Aileen tells Nan. 'The pilot landed in the pub carpark then ran up the hill with them under his arm, for the day's briefing. The place was full of firefighters. Now it's mostly full of locals, as you can see. We've brought in some of the seniors, too. Just in case. Figured it was easier to keep an eye on them here. Ted and Pearl won't budge, but their neighbours are looking out for them.'

The radio blares constantly and people shout over the sound. There's also the noise of aircraft – helicopters returning to refuel, small float planes scooping water from the lake. Tye notices that the fire updates seem to be getting more frequent – every twenty minutes or so. The guy in charge strides out of the office, phone at his ear. He paces the length of the hall, talking intently, then is gone again.

Lance sits on the back veranda out of the wind, catching up with an old fishing mate he hasn't seen for years. A situation like this brings everyone out of the woodwork.

Tye hands them each a cup of tea as a huge chopper comes in to land.

'They're bringing in the big guns,' Lance's mate yells. 'That's a Black Hawk. Ex-US military.'

Nan appears at the door. 'I hope Barry doesn't see that one,' she shouts to Tye. 'That's where all his troubles started.'

Tye would like to ask what Nan means but she doesn't get the chance.

'Vietnam,' Lance tells her.

She follows Nan inside. Her grandmother's phone never stops. Thirty calls so far. Tye's keeping count. Community members with a thousand enquiries.

'Not at the moment, June,' Nan's saying. 'We'll know more after the meeting . . . yes, late this afternoon. Can we count on you to be here?'

Lunch, then afternoon tea for the oldies and it's getting close to the time for the community meeting.

'Top up the urn, will you, love?' Aileen asks Tye. 'And could you start putting out the chairs.'

'How many?'

'All of them. Should get a good turnout. Everyone's worried.'

Tye is setting out the first row when two stocky little kids burst into the hall, kick off their shoes and slide across the floor in their socks, whooping and yelling. One crashes into the chair Tye's just put down and knocks it over. A tall, grouchy-looking man with white hair picks it up and plonks himself in it, folding his arms over his belly.

'Ray,' a woman calls. 'Look after those kids, will you. I'm going to start packing.'

'Panic merchant!' he shouts after her departing figure.

The double doors swing shut, then open again as a police officer walks in. Tye watches as the tall man immediately collars him.

'Brendan. Just the fellow I want to see.'

'Later,' the policeman says, giving a curt nod before ducking into the control room.

The chairs quickly fill. People are keen to find out what's going on. Where exactly are the fires at this point? Which way are they heading? Should we stay or leave? people ask. Could Merrick really be under threat?

Lily arrives and hurries over to Tye. 'Did you go and see him?' she asks.

Tye shakes her head. 'Didn't get the chance.'

Lily picks up a stack of chairs and starts helping. When one of the rampaging kids collides with her she puts down the chairs and grabs him. Then she squats and looks him in the eye. Tye doesn't hear what she says, but the boy slinks away with a resentful look and slumps down in the front row. He picks up a pamphlet from the chair seat and begins tearing it into strips. His sister trundles over and joins him.

'Ray Salter's grandkids,' Lil tells Tye. 'Mum delivered both of them when she worked at the General. They're shockers. Mum calls them the bruisers.'

Tye laughs.

'Are you evacuating?' Lil asks. 'Mum wants me to go. I want to stay.'

'Go where?'

Lily shrugs. 'Not sure yet. Maybe my cousin's place in Ouse. Mum's worried about the animals, too. She's going to ask your nan if we can borrow the mail van. That's if we need to leave.'

'But the fire's nowhere near us.' Tye points to the big screen on the wall. 'It's miles away from Chancy's.'

Tye's studied that screen, over and over, checking out the icons, the warning levels – yellow flames for Advice, orange for Watch and Act, red for Emergency. The burnt areas are shown in grey and the shapes keep changing as the information is updated. One part looks like a dog with an open mouth, another, a finger pointing south. The finger gets longer. Meanwhile, the flank of the fire is travelling slowly west towards the national park, and the alpine areas where the pencil pines grow. She remembers Kelly-Ann's photos and shuts her eyes tight. 'It's not coming this way, Lil,' she says. 'Not towards Merrick.'

'Get real, Tye. Uranus makes everything unpredictable.'

Tye looks around the hall. It's rapidly filling and firefighters are starting to come in, having finished their shift. A woman arrives and collapses in a chair inside the door. She's so blackened from smoke and fire-dust Tye can barely make out her uniform. When Aileen goes to greet her she gives a weary smile and closes her eyes, resting her head against the wall.

Tye sees Kay come in with some of the crew. No sign of Pop yet. He might be on a different truck. Then Tye feels a hand on her shoulder.

'Saved me a seat, did you?'

'Kelly-Ann! When did you get here?' Tye says. 'How's it looking?'

'Rugged,' Kel replies. 'We're all flat chat. But anyone who could be spared is coming in for the meeting. Communication is the key. Important we're all on the same page.'

'Are the pines okay?'

'So far, touch wood.' Kelly-Ann taps the floorboards and plonks into a plastic chair. 'Our containment lines are holding. We've put in rows of sprinklers.'

The radio is turned off, someone hands out pamphlets and Kay introduces the first speaker, a man from the Tasmania Fire Service who has driven down from Launceston.

'The winds are erratic. Choppy north-westerlies with gusts up to eighty kays. There's no saying what will happen in the next few days, but the forecast for the weekend is worrying. Places potentially at risk include Shannon, Penstock Lagoon and Waddamana. And Merrick, of course. So, we're advising everyone to be ready to leave. The safest option is to go early. Don't wait to see what happens. Have water, blankets and a torch in the car and make sure the road is clear before you set off. Evacuation centres are being set up in Deloraine and Bothwell.' He holds up a bunch of cards. 'If you go, you'll need a resident's pass to get back in. The highway will be closed to everyone but locals. Forms are on the table.'

'Hold it right there.'

Ray Salter is on his feet. A collective groan passes through the crowd.

'What about looters? I'm not leaving my property unattended. A mate of mine got his boat pinched from Craig's Bay just a few days ago. Brand new outboard on it too. I wanted to talk to you about it, Brendan.'

'I know, Ray. It's been reported,' Brendan says.

'Well, what are you doing about it?'

The policeman takes Ray Salter aside and the meeting continues.

'Some of you may want to stay and defend,' the speaker says. 'We advise against it but it's up to you to decide. You'll have to be well prepared. You need the right gear – goggles, gloves, a broad-brimmed hat to protect you from falling embers. Strong boots and a long-sleeved shirt, heavy cotton if possible. Plus you'll need a fire pump and fire hoses. Your garden hose won't cut it. You should be strong and physically fit. And mentally prepared as well. The racket of the aircraft today is nothing compared with the roar of an approaching fire. If you're not a hundred per cent confident, leave. We don't want to be rescuing you in the middle of an emergency.'

Tye looks to the back of the hall and sees Pop has arrived. He's standing with other firefighters and is covered in soot and ash. She's never seen him look so grim.

The man speaking is now pointing to a map. 'If the fire jumps the River Ouse you'll get an alarm on your phone.' He brings up Merrick on the screen and starts talking about the most vulnerable areas, the shacks on the western flank of the settlement. 'We'll finish back-burning tomorrow.'

Tye isn't really taking it in. One of the bruisers, the boy, has helped himself to a pile of pamphlets from the information table and, with surprising dexterity, is making paper planes. His sister watches keenly.

'There are fifty fires burning around the state today,' the TFS fellow says. 'Twenty thousand hectares have been burnt in the south-west wilderness area, the Gell River fire is still going, and the Huon Valley is under increasing threat.' He pauses and looks steadily into the audience. 'So far no properties have been lost. We hope to keep it that way. But the situation is rapidly changing, especially here in the Highlands.'

Lily leans towards Tye. 'Do they know how many animals have been lost?' she whispers.

Tye shakes her head.

'Five more came in today,' Lily tells her. 'I don't know how Mum's going to cope.'

'Burnt?' Tye asks.

'Burnt, injured, orphaned. That's why I need to stay here and help Mum.'

Tye decides she needs to stay as well. She's thinking of Bailey, alone in the shack waiting for his uncle.

Her thoughts are interrupted when she's hit by a flying missile. She stares daggers at Ray Salter's grandson, then picks up the paper plane and unfolds it to read the heading.

Bushfire Survival Plan.

Tye shivers, in spite of the heat.

Ten

'**Never seen the likes of it,**' Pop says on the way home. 'How long have I been fighting fires, darl?'

'More than thirty years – closer to forty,' Nan replies. 'We've got the extra beds ready for the crew flying in.'

'Good,' Pop says. 'I think we'll put the New Zealanders in there tonight. Then work out where everyone will go tomorrow when the others arrive from the mainland.'

'Tye, you might lose your cabin for a couple of days,' Nan adds. 'Okay by you?'

'Back behind the curtain, then?'

'Well, maybe. But I think it'd be better if you go and stay on the farm with your Auntie Jill until things settle a bit.'

'I'd rather stay here,' Tye says.

Nan seems not to have heard. 'We'll take you down first thing tomorrow,' she announces.

'I agree with your nan,' Pop adds. 'There's no immediate danger at Chancy's but it would put our minds at rest.'

Soon after they get home the first group of visiting firefighters arrives.

In spite of Pop's reassurance Tye feels anxious, and she knows she can't go off to Jill's without seeing Bailey first. She seizes her chance while Nan is busy with the newcomers.

'Just going down to the water for a bit,' she tells Pop.

'Good idea. It's cooling down now. Don't be long though.'

Tye takes some things from the guests' kitchen. There's not much there – a bit of leftover rice, some dry biscuits. She grabs what she can find and gets on the bike. It's seven o'clock and the wind has dropped. The lake is stained indigo in the evening light and the far shore is lost in a blue haze of smoke.

What she has to tell Bailey isn't going to be easy. Tye goes over it in her mind, trying to think what to say. *Bailey, about your Uncle Reg . . . I'm sorry but . . .* She wishes Lil was with her.

Bailey is right where they left him, sitting in front of the shack, watching Wanda graze. When he sees Tye he jumps to his feet, all smiles. He looks heaps better than when she last saw him – the food, she guesses, plus having friends.

'Guess what, Tye?' He runs towards her. 'Wanda's learned a trick. We've been practising it. You should see—'

Bailey stops midstride. 'What is it? What's wrong?'

'There's something I have to tell you.' Tye gulps. *Better sit him down,* she thinks, and taking the food from her basket, she walks to the step.

Bailey remains standing. He looks worried. 'Where's that other girl?'

'She couldn't come. She has to go away. Because of the fires. I have to, as well.'

'Where?'

'To my auntie's place down near Bothwell.'

'When will you be back?'

'Not sure. In a day or so, I guess.'

'Well, that's okay,' he says. 'By then the old bloke might—'

Tye takes a deep breath. There's no gentle way to tell him the bad news. 'Bailey, your Uncle Reg isn't coming back.'

'Why not?'

'He died.'

Bailey pales beneath his sunburn. He frowns, and for a moment his face seems to crumple. Then he bites his lip and stares at Tye fiercely. 'He didn't,' he mutters. Picking up Wanda, he steps past Tye and goes into the shack. 'That's a lie!'

Tye gets up and follows him. She stands at the door. Bailey's sitting on the floor, leaning against the couch and holding Wanda close.

'It's true, Bailey,' she says quietly.

'Well, nobody told *me*.'

'Maybe they didn't know.'

Bailey begins rocking Wanda in his arms. He keeps clearing his throat as if something's stuck in it. When Tye puts her hand on his arm, he shakes it off.

'You can't stay here by yourself,' she says. 'Come with

me. I'm sure my grandparents can help you out. They could fix things up for you.'

Bailey shakes his head. Then, with Wanda under his arm, he leans over a battered carton and starts pulling things out – tattered car manuals, a sheaf of yellow letters half-eaten by silverfish, an old road map that's coming apart at the folds.

He stares at the map for a long time, then says, 'I'll go to the bunker. Reckon I can find it now. Just need to get to the turnoff before the pub.'

'Bailey, the fires . . . And what about Auntie Bev? When you don't come home from camp? You should call her.'

'I can't. Don't you understand anything?'

'It's not safe,' Tye says.

'Neither's Barton Hall. Or sharing a room with Carter,' he mutters, turning away. 'Plenty of food and other stuff in that bunker. Fifty years' worth.'

He keeps going through the carton. After a while it seems he's forgotten Tye's there. She slips outside, walks out of earshot and phones Lily. 'He says he'll go to that bunker,' she says quietly.

'No way!' Lil cries. 'Tell him to go to Barry's.'

That might work. Barry's his uncle's friend.

'I'll try.'

Tye returns to the shack and finds Bailey standing at the door, clutching Wanda. He looks vaguely in her direction, stroking the joey in a distracted way. He still has the map in his hand.

'What about going to Barry's?' she says. 'He was a

good mate of your uncle's. He might even be pleased to see you.'

Bailey shrugs. He gazes into the smoky sky for a minute and then he slips the map in his back pocket. 'Guess I'll have to.'

When Tye returns to Chancy's, her grandparents are sitting down to eat. Tye shakes her head when Nan offers her the dish of cauliflower cheese. She sits at the table, silent.

'What's up?' Nan asks. 'Cat got your tongue?'

Tye says nothing. She doesn't trust herself to speak. If she does she might say too much, give the whole game away.

Eleven

Tye feels as if she has arrived on another planet. The air is hot and smoky, the Studleyvale phone rings constantly and neighbouring property owners keep dropping in to tee-up fire preparations with Jill. There's talk of moving valuable breeding stock and deciding what gates will be left open if the worst happens. Some farmers are moving tractors and machinery out of the implement sheds and parking them on worked ground. Others are moving fuel tanks; they don't want diesel stored near the outbuildings. Some discuss widening existing firebreaks but they're worried about leaving debris on the ground. They offer each other advice. Tye listens to it all but it's not the same as being at the heart of the action.

She wishes she were at the Merrick community hall, helping Nan. Reports of fires keep coming in but the threat seems less real down here on the farm. Trying to picture what's happening sixty kilometres up the road is like trying to see through fog or smoke and getting only shadowy glimpses of what's beyond. Even the sounds of the helicopters and the drone of fire trucks on the nearby highway seem less urgent here than they had around Merrick. Tye wishes Nan and Pop had let her stay at home, but they'd made it clear no negotiation was possible. It was probably the same for Lily.

Jill goes about the farm work with calm efficiency. 'Doesn't panic easily,' Tye has often heard Pop say, about his sister. 'Just gets on with it.' *And expects me to as well*, Tye thinks.

She has barely unpacked her things when Jill is at her bedroom door, sleeves rolled up to her elbows, dusty boots, and weathered face damp with sweat. 'Might as well lend a hand while you're here, Tye. We need to move the ewes down to the home paddock. Not that the fire is likely to come this far, but best to be prepared. I'll get Tilly and Jack. See you out the front.'

Ten minutes later Jill pulls up on an ag-bike and gives instructions. 'If you wouldn't mind opening that second gate.' She points across the bare paddock to a fenceline beyond the sheds. 'Pick you up there in five.' She whistles and two border collies appear from nowhere, barking and eager.

Tye starts walking across the paddock. It's still early but heat is radiating from the bare ground.

'Hat!' Jill yells above the sound of the engine, pointing back to the house. Then she speeds off in the opposite direction.

Tye grabs a hat from the hat stand in the hall rather than go upstairs to get her own. She hurries towards the gate. Her auntie's already there, waiting with the dogs.

'That's Dad's hat,' Jill says, laughing.

My great-grandfather, Tye thinks. She opens the gate and gets on behind Jill, who nods towards the foothills. 'We're bringing them back from the bush block.' The dogs streak ahead and Jill and Tye roar after them.

Tye used to love the farm. She has memories of the shearing shed and the big snowy fleeces being flung out on a table. They pass the sheep yards and head up a lane between some paddocks beyond the riverflats. The hat is far too big and Tye has to hold it on.

'Both hands,' Jill yells, as the track gets rougher. They bounce over some tree roots and Tye loses the hat. Shortly after, Jill pulls up at a gate near some big old eucalypts. Tye gets off to open it and Jill rides on alone. Soon she's out of sight. Tye hears the occasional whistle and shout, then the barking of the dogs grows faint.

She goes back for the hat, a greasy old thing, hardly a family heirloom. Puts it on and sits in the shade. She already feels windburnt from the ride. She thinks of Bailey. She could have put some sunscreen in that food bag.

Tye wonders if she did the right thing by telling Lily about him. After all, she'd made a promise. But together they'd come up with a plan for Bailey. He's probably with Barry right now, at least Tye hopes so.

There's a hot wind blowing from the north and the trees are thrashing about. Perhaps she shouldn't be sitting beneath them.

By the time Tye hears the bike again, along with the bleating of sheep, she's hot and thirsty.

'If we've missed a few they'll have to take their chances,' Jill says as Tilly and Jack shepherd the mob through the gate. Tye closes it behind them.

'Thanks for helping,' Jill says, when the sheep are in the home paddock. 'Take a break. Get yourself a cool drink, and do your own thing for an hour or so while I check the troughs and pumps.'

Tye wipes the sweat from her brow. She returns to the homestead, puts her great-grandfather's hat back on the hook and goes to check on her pencil pine seedling – she brought it with her, and she's decided the bathroom is closest to its natural environment. The stone house is remarkably cool and the bathroom is coolest of all, being on the south side. She puts the seedling in a tray of water beside the washbasin, tops it up, then goes to the kitchen for a drink.

There's a laptop open on the bench. Jill comes in, downs two glasses of water and puts on the kettle.

'What's the latest?' she asks.

Tye scrolls the TFS site and her aunt looks over her shoulder.

'It's getting a bit too close to Merrick for comfort,' Jill says. 'Hope people have the sense to get out before they're trapped. But your nan and pop are old hands. At least we know they won't do anything stupid.'

'Not like the stupid things people have been doing for centuries,' Tye blurts out. 'Trashing the planet, making species extinct and causing bigger and fiercer bushfires that wipe out vulnerable plants like pencil pines and cider gums. The Aboriginal people looked after the land for thousands of years but look what's happened in the last two hundred years.'

She wonders where the outburst came from. Perhaps she's more worried than she'd care to admit.

Jill puts up her hand. 'That sort of talk gets us nowhere. We've just got to concentrate on what we're facing right now.'

They hear a vehicle pull up and Jill heads outside. Tye looks out the window. It's Rick Peters, from Honeywood, the next farm. Jill stands talking to him for ages. Tye's curiosity — and her fear — are aroused. When he leaves, Tye hurries out.

'Idiots,' Jill's muttering.

'What did Mr Peters want?' Tye asks. 'Has he heard from his son?' Jason Peters and his wife Maree are one of the Merrick families who've decided to stay and defend.

'The evacuation's been on the news,' Jill tells her. 'They're saying everyone's gone, that Merrick's a ghost town, except for the fire station and the hall. You know what that means, don't you?'

Tye shakes her head.

'Looters.' Jill folds her arms. 'As if the police haven't got enough to do. And, Jason says some drongos are out fishing on the lakes, right where the helicopters are scooping up water. Where do these people keep their brains, you wonder? Just clueless!'

Jill watches the vehicle disappear up the drive, then strides away. Tye trails back inside, out of the heat and blustery wind. *Better let Mum know where I am,* she thinks. But Opal's not answering.

Soon Jill calls from outside. 'Can you give me a hand, Tye?'

One job follows the next. Tye doesn't mind the work. Being busy helps to keep her mind off the fire and from fretting about her family's safety. Keeps her mind off Bailey as well. She wonders how long his food will last. Once he runs out he'll go to Barry, she tells herself. Barry will know what happened with his uncle. Bailey's probably having lunch with him right now. But somehow she can't see it.

By midday it's too hot to be outside and Tye finds herself alone in the kitchen.

What about Barry's dogs, she wonders. Do they know Bailey? How long since he was last at his uncle's shack? It could have been years ago. She really doesn't know much about Bailey at all. And yet she feels responsible for him. She texts Lily: Do the dogs know Bailey? They look savage . . . There's no reply, so Tye calls. Phone is either turned off or out of range. *Great,* she thinks. *Mercury retro, as Lil would say.*

Soon enough Jill calls out again for help. Tye focuses on one task after the other. Then her phone sounds. It's Opal and she's in frantic mother mode.

'What's going on? I just heard about the fires. Where are you? Are you in danger? Put Mum on. I need to speak to her, pronto. Or Dad.'

Tye sighs. 'They're not here. Pop's out fighting fires. Nan's up at Merrick feeding the firefighters and

I'm down at Studleyvale with Auntie Jill. The fires are nowhere near here. Nowhere near Chancy's either.'

'I thought you'd be safe down there at the ends of the earth. I want you out of there, Tye, do you hear me?'

Tye holds the phone away from her ear till the worst of Opal's tirade is over. As soon as Opal hangs up, Tye calls Nan's mobile. No answer. So she tries the hall number and gets Aileen.

'Tye?' Aileen says. 'You're after your nan? She's outside, unloading supplies. Probably didn't hear your call. There's a fair din going on here.'

'Just tell her my mum called,' Tye says, 'and she's on the warpath.'

'Done,' Aileen replies.

A few minutes later Jas calls. Jas is so much easier to talk to than Opal. It's not all about what *she* wants. Jas actually listens. 'I'm glad you're safe,' she says.

Tye can hear relief in Jas's voice.

'Can you get Mum off my back?' Tye begs.

Jas laughs. 'I'll try to call her. I'll admit she can be a bit intense.'

'A bit! She's demanding I fly home immediately. She's about to book me a ticket.'

Jas laughs again. 'I understand why she's worried – we both are – but she's never been one for half measures, our Opal. I'll try to rein her in. But I don't like my chances.'

The endless day drags on, Tye checking the fire reports over and over.

Jill comes in late, dead tired, to say goodnight and to tell Tye that a dozen fireys will be arriving later that night, to be billeted here. They'll stay in the shearers' quarters. Jill will provide breakfast, and the local pub will prepare cut lunches and their evening meal.

Tye's stomach clenches. The arrival of more firefighters must mean things are getting worse. But there's no point in plaguing her aunt with questions.

When Tye goes to bed she can't sleep for worrying. Chancy's is not in the fire zone. Nan is safe at the hall, surrounded by firefighters and Lance'll be with her but what about Pop and Kay and the others? How would it be out there on the frontline, facing walls of flames? And what about Bailey? Maybe she should call Barry Saunders to make sure the boy's all right. But Barry's a hermit – he mightn't even have a phone. If he has, would the number be listed? Nan would know but she can't ask Nan. Tye sits up in bed and scrolls the white pages, searching for Barry's number. She's surprised when she finds it. Right, she'll call him. But not this late. Tomorrow morning, as soon as it's light.

She snaps off the light, glad to see the end of this day.

Twelve

By sunrise, it's too hot to sleep. Tye wakes with a start. Reaches for her phone. Thumbs in Barry's number. It rings and rings. At last a grumpy voice says, 'Yeah?'

'Barry? Mr Saunders? It's Tyenna, Rob and Lena's granddaughter.'

Harsh coughing sounds on the other end of the phone.

Tye is suddenly aware of the time. 'Sorry to call you so early, but do you know ... I mean, I was wondering ... is Bailey Stokes there with you?'

'That little ratbag! He did come nosing round here, but I sent him packing. Got no patience with runaways. Before you know it, you find yourself tangled up with police and social workers. I told him to get lost. Get himself back to Launceston quick smart.'

There's the sound of furious barking and then the phone goes dead.

Stung by Barry's words, Tye steps out onto the veranda into an eerie half-light. The harsh smell of smoke is everywhere. Her eyes sting and her throat closes. In the home paddock the sheep are milling about restlessly. As Tye watches, a mob of fireys spills out of the bunkhouse. They scramble into their gear, then leap into their trucks, which cross the grid with a shuddering clang and head for the highway.

Behind her the local radio station is spewing the latest reports. *Things are reaching desperation point near the Central Highlands town of Merrick. Conditions are described as horrendous. And with strong winds pushing the fire towards the township there appears to be no way Merrick can survive. Eyewitnesses report crowns of eucalypts exploding and sending fireballs into the air and embers as big as outstretched hands landing up to ten kilometres ahead of the fire-front.*

Tye steps back inside and flicks on the TV as well. Sees images of smoke and flames roaring into orange and black skies. Fire trucks engulfed in oily billows of smoke and helmeted figures in their yellow gear pointing hoses into storeys-high flames. Is Pop among them? She searches the screen for a glimpse of him. She hopes Bailey has taken Barry's advice and headed for Launceston. He'd have to go via Deloraine and not through Merrick. Would he even score a lift, she wonders, looking as scruffy as he does?

Auntie Jill strides in from the veranda and nods towards the blaring TV. 'It's going to be a pretty full-on day by the looks of that. But don't upset yourself by watching all the horror over and over again.'

She begins to tidy the kitchen, then stops and turns to Tye. 'Are you okay?'

Tye tries to answer but the words stick in her throat. She starts to shake.

'No – not really,' she finally manages to say.

Jill draws her onto the old settee in the corner of the kitchen.

'Now listen to me,' she says. 'I know you're frightened. We all are. Where bushfires are concerned you'd be foolish not to be. But you can be sure everyone's doing their best—'

'But Pop, and Nan too . . .' Maybe Nan's not safe after all.

Tears gather in the corners of her eyes and her head swims. Jill puts an arm round her.

'Your nan's fine,' Jill tells Tye. 'She rang from the hall. Said not to wake you. Most of the locals who stayed are there as well. She got through from Chancy's all right, long before dawn. Brought Lance with her. Said it was pretty smoky on the way down, embers flying everywhere. She reckoned there were forty-eight fire trucks in the pub carpark when she arrived, all with their noses pointing out, ready to roll. Your pop and his crew, and all the others. They didn't waste any time; it was action stations from the word go. Pretty soon you could hardly hear over the racket of planes and helicopters. But don't you worry. They're well trained. They know what they're doing. Rob's an old hand. Been fighting fires since he was nearly as young as you.'

Tye barely nods. Her head feels like it's going to explode. But she mustn't lose it when everyone else is doing their bit. She tells herself, of course, they'll be all right.

She sniffs back her tears and gives her aunt a weak grin. 'Sorry.'

'Perfectly understandable.' Jill's all brisk and business-like again. 'If you're okay I'll push on with things.'

As soon as Jill leaves the kitchen, Tye's back at the computer, checking the warnings and scanning the latest updates. There are fires burning on a number of fronts now, but the one near Merrick is the scariest. It's almost at the town. She swallows a lump in her throat and tries to tell herself not to worry. People in the bush are used to fires. The fireys have decades of experience. And help has come from all over. The helicopters and planes can dump tonnes of water in one go. If only the wind would die down, or change direction.

When Jill returns, her face is grave. 'It looks like touch and go, at this stage. But they'll give it their best shot. You can be sure of that. Only thing to do now is get some food into us and be ready to act if we need to.'

She reaches into the fridge and pulls out a carton of eggs. Soon the aroma of scrambled eggs fills the air. Tye cuts thick slabs of bread and drops them into the toaster. She's trying to rein in her panicky thoughts. What if the fires wipe out Merrick, then keep going? They're everywhere, it seems. They might spread all across the plateau, wipe out the alpine forests. She wants to believe Auntie Jill, but it's hard to keep her feelings under control.

Get a grip! She's always been praised for being a calm and capable girl, and this is certainly not the time to lose her cool!

Updates come in every ten minutes or so, each one more frightening than the last. Firefighters are struggling to defend the town. People are in danger of losing their properties, even their lives. Jill and Tye check the TFS website again and again. The fire has reached Merrick, one report says, and crews are foaming the shacks and houses in a desperate attempt to save them. Another mentions the possibility that several of the fire fronts may join up, in the days to come, and, worst-case scenario, create a mega firestorm. Some of the reports seem to contradict one another. There's no way of knowing which are right.

Tye hears nothing from Nan all day. Her grandmother is too flat out to call, she realises. She hears nothing from Pop either. Her fingers itch to call him, but she mustn't, she knows that. There's probably no reception where he is, and anyway he'd never hear the phone over the racket of the fire.

Opal calls again, her voice shrill with panic. Tye can't listen. She rushes into the bathroom to splash some cool water on her face and that's when the dreadful mishap occurs. Her elbow catches the plant pot and before she can steady it, her pencil pine seedling is dashed to the floor.

'No-o-oh!' she cries, falling to her knees. She scoops the pot up, rights the seedling then scrapes up the soil and pats it tenderly back around the little plant. One of the branches is a bit bent, but other than that the seedling has come to no harm.

But it's too much for Tye. She bursts into tears. The world is on fire, and she can't even take care of one small plant. She totally loses it then. Sobs in a heap on the bathroom floor for what seems forever.

The storm of tears is starting to subside when her phone rings. It's Opal – for the third time. Tye slides her phone off and shoves it into her pocket. She doesn't need Opal's panic added to her own. There's nothing her mum can do from Queensland about her situation, just as there's no way Tye can know from Studleyvale whether Nan and Pop are safe. And then there's Bailey . . . She pushes him out of her mind.

It's not till late in the afternoon that they learn that the winds have swung around. It looks like the town will be saved.

'It was a close shave,' Jill tells Tye. 'The fire burned right to the backyards of houses and shacks on the town boundaries. They foamed the buildings and luckily the firebreaks held. There'll be plenty of horror stories, from those on the frontline. But the firefighters did a wonderful job and no people or buildings were lost, except for a single farmhouse out on the plains.'

Jill's sighing with relief. Tye is relieved too, but she won't be happy till she hears from Pop.

The long day finally drags to a close. It's nearly midnight before a text comes from Nan. We made it. Then another, a row of xxxxs from Pop.

Tye texts back: When can I come home?

We'll see, is the reply.

'Bed!' Jill abruptly announces. 'We need some rest, to be fighting fit for what tomorrow may bring.'

But Tye can't rest. All day she's been blocking thoughts of Bailey, and when she lies down they come rushing in. What if he didn't go to Launceston? Why would he when Carter's at Auntie Bev's? What if he tried to reach the bunker he'd told them about? The turn-off was before Merrick. No, he would have seen smoke and heard sirens and with so many police around he'd be lying low. He's probably at the shack waiting for her.

Tye pulls up the sheet. It's so hot that's all the bedding she needs. She tosses and turns.

What if Bailey's out there somewhere? No one but she and Lily would know. And Lily's in Ouse, out of reach. It'll be Tye's fault if anything happens to him. She should have told Nan and Pop about him from the start. She should never have kept him secret. Tye closes her eyes and wills her thoughts to stop.

It takes ages to get to sleep and when she finally dozes off, her dreams are troubled by images of flickering flames. She sees a lone figure running, running and getting nowhere. She calls to him to come back, but no sound comes out, and when she tries to race after him, her legs won't move – something is tethering her to the spot. The figure gets further away and smaller and smaller and finally disappears.

Tye wakes in the dark with her heart pounding and her head full of questions. What if Bailey made his way to the turn-off before the fires came close? How far did yesterday's fires reach? She checks the time: 2 a.m. Creeps out into the kitchen. Where exactly is that bunker?

Her face glows in the light of the laptop. She googles, and finds it on a property that used to be called

Sheenroan. But it's a wreck. A total dump. Crumbling concrete and twisted iron – it looks like some sort of gaol. It was someone's idea of safety, once, she discovers as she reads the text. An American billionaire had it built in the 1970s and fitted it out as a nuclear shelter. His safe hideout in case of war and devastation. A refuge. It's about twenty kilometres southwest of Merrick by road, less as the crow flies.

Then she looks up the fire maps. Merrick is safe. She can see where the fire stopped right at the town's edge but black areas stretch beyond its boundaries. Many of those are still burning, she can tell by the icons. She takes a deep breath and follows the highway south. Closes one window and opens another. Jumps across to Google Earth, finds the highway again. Veers to the west and zooms in, and further in.

There aren't many named roads down that way, just old forestry trails and farm tracks. Maybe it's pure chance but she finds Sheenroan Road. It follows a river, then winds up through forested land, disappearing from sight before emerging to cross an open area – a swamp, perhaps, or at least it was when these satellite photos were taken.

Tye feels she's travelling across country. She zooms in until she can't go any closer. Obviously marshlands, she persuades herself; bright green and nowhere near the fires. She almost expects to see Bailey on the road. Then slowly Sheenroan Road disappears in a series of braided tracks. She zooms out, closes her eyes and memorises the area.

When Tye tabs back to the fire map her heart sinks. The country near Sheenroan isn't grey on the TFS website but there's no way Bailey could have reached it without passing through the fire front. Tye drops her head. She's made a foolish misjudgement. And now it's too late. She wishes everything could go back to before the bushfire. It feels like a lifetime ago.

She looks back at the screen, returns to the site of the ruined bunker. The billionaire's bolthole. Bailey's too. But there's no way it could shelter him now, even if he could reach it safely.

Some animals run into the fire, she knows. They leap through the flames rather than try to outrun them. Jump through the fire front to the safety of burnt ground. *Not people*, Tye thinks. *Not Bailey*. He's a bush kid – that was clear from the start. He's not a fool. He wouldn't run before the fires and he wouldn't jump through them. He would keep himself safe and keep Wanda safe as well.

But in the middle of the night your thoughts run like startled creatures. They race in all directions. As Tye's do, till the grey dawn breaks. Half asleep, she reaches for her phone. Instinctively taps OPAL. A few seconds later, her mum's message begins, *Hi, it's Opal I can't—* Tye presses JAS, changes her mind, shuts the phone off and stumbles out of bed.

Thirteen

When Tye goes to the kitchen her aunt looks worn out. 'Hardly got a wink of sleep,' she says. 'Maybe it was relief. Saw your light was on. Nearly brought you a hot drink.'

'We'll all sleep well tonight, Auntie Jill.'

'That's if we get a break.' Jill's on the laptop, scrolling. 'The temperatures are looking better and the wind has dropped. That's something. Your nan says she woke up cold and had to get a blanket. Crazy, isn't it.'

Tye looks out the window. The trucks of the visiting fireys are still parked outside the shearers' quarters.

'Lena will be down soon to pick you up. Lily too. Carla's sister is dropping her off.'

Jill turns to Tye. 'Breakfast?'

Tye's stomach's churning. 'I'll eat when I get home, thanks.'

She packs her bag and collects her seedling.

A message arrives from Lily. Got your texts. Ouse dead boring. CU soon.

'I really appreciated your help,' Jill says as they head out onto the veranda. 'Next time you come, let's hope it can be more of a holiday.'

When Nan arrives, Tye runs down the steps and gives her a big hug. Nan holds her for a long time. Now's the moment to lay down her burden. She's about to tell everything when she looks up and sees tears in her grandmother's eyes.

'Close call, eh?' Jill says.

Nan turns to Jill and shakes her head. They start talking about Merrick's near miss and the moment passes.

Tye texts Lil, He's not with Barry. Lil replies, He's at the shack? Tye sends an emoji – fingers crossed. She's glad to be back in contact with her friend. It's been a long couple of days with Lil out of range.

Lily arrives then, and soon they're heading north. Nan has a resident's pass propped on the dashboard and she drives slowly. Tye watches the road ahead.

'Poor Mum,' Lily says. 'You wouldn't believe how many animals have come in.'

'And the fires aren't over,' Nan tells them. 'Not by a long shot. Chancy's is full now and will be for as long as it takes. The girls from the Remote Area Team are in your cabin, Tye, so you'll be back in the cubby.'

Tye pulls down the sun visor and she and Lily exchange a glance. Injured animals are not their only worry.

Blackened trees line both sides of the road. A few kilometres on, there's a roadblock. Brendan is standing beside his police car. 'Oh, it's you, Lena,' he says as he flags them down. 'Sorry. Didn't recognise the ute, for a minute.'

'Aileen's got the van,' she tells him. 'She'll be down directly to pick up supplies.'

'Is everyone all right?' Brendan asks. He looks worn out.

'Fine,' says Nan. 'Just a bit shaken.'

'Me too, but we're safe for now. Nothing left to burn, eh, not around Merrick anyway.'

Tye pictures the bunker, then immediately blocks the thought. She looks at the seedling on her lap and thinks instead of trees. 'What about the Walls?' she asks. 'Did the fire get up there?'

As she speaks a huge plane roars overhead, grey as ash and gaining height. Brendan shouts over the sound. 'That's the Hercules, for protecting the national park. As far as I know everything is all right. For the moment anyway. Things keep changing.'

The air booms with the plane's passing.

'But Chancy's is fine, isn't it?' Lily says.

'Yep. Well out of it, at this stage. But who can say? Keep listening to the radio.' He pauses. Somewhere a tree groans, cracks and falls with a dull thud. Then a chainsaw starts up. 'Drive safely,' Brendan says, and waves them on.

There are a couple of cars in front, travelling slowly like Nan, and the journey feels like a procession. Tye has only ever been to one funeral in her life, an acquaintance of Opal's. She doesn't remember whose it was – she was only little. The drive back up to the plateau makes her think of that time.

The trees are black silhouettes and, in places, incinerated stumps rise from thick beds of ash. Fences are burnt and strands of blackened wire dangle from the occasional post. There are animals on the roadside. A straggly sheep in full wool runs away as they pass, raising little puffs of ash. A cow is standing next to the sections of a log that has recently been cut. The tree must have fallen across the road. The cow solemnly stares as they drive on.

Tye sees some cider gums standing in a burnt paddock. Without their leaves the magnificent trees look tormented, a tangle of writhing branches.

'It'll all grow back,' Nan says. 'This time next year you won't know the place.'

Tye knows that's not completely true.

'You're quiet,' Nan remarks. 'How did you go at Jill's? Did she wear you out?'

Tye mumbles something about being kept busy. She glances at Lily, then gazes through the passenger window. Everything looks black and white, like an old movie. No blue in the sky and no green on the ground. If she thought the area behind Chancy's carpark was a war zone when she first arrived from Melbourne, it's nothing compared with this.

'Look!' Lily cries. 'Lena, stop!'

A big wombat is sitting by the roadside, so still it might have been a boulder. Then another one. And another.

When Nan pulls up Lily jumps out and rushes back to the nearest wombat. Tye puts the seedling on the seat and runs after her.

'Dead,' Lily says. She feels inside the pouch but it's empty. 'Come on, let's check the others.'

Lil slips her arm through Tye's and hurries on. 'How do you know he didn't go to Barry's?' she whispers.

'He went, but Barry sent him away. I called him.'

Lily looks scared. 'This is so textbook Uranus,' she says, biting her lip. 'But don't worry, the fire didn't go anywhere near the shack.'

'But what if he went to the bunker?' Tye holds her friend tight. She's sick with worry, ready to throw up.

The next wombat is dead too, and so is the third one. The girls blink back tears, their eyes hot.

'We shouldn't have kept him secret, Tye. Not with Pluto in the mix. You can't mess with Pluto.'

The mention of astrology brings Tye back to earth. No point in jumping to conclusions, she tells herself.

'We'll go to the shack first. If he's not there we have to tell someone.'

Lil looks down at the dead wombat and nods. 'Male,' she says. 'No pouch to check.'

'Not a mark on them,' Lily tells Nan when they return to the ute. 'It must have been the smoke. At least there's no young.'

The next wombat they pass isn't dead. It's not even hurt, just stunned. 'Can you help me lift him into the back?' Lily says.

The animal is huge and it takes the three of them to pick him up. He doesn't protest. The girls try to make the wombat comfortable, putting him against the cab and placing their bags behind him to stop him sliding back. Now Nan drives even slower, trying to avoid the bumps.

Then Lily spots a wallaby. 'There!' she calls out. 'Stop!'

'I'm sorry, Lil,' Nan says. 'We can't collect animals and carry them loose in the tray. Call your mum. Tell her she can take the van once Aileen brings it back.'

Lily phones Carla. 'It's terrible, Mum,' they hear her wail. 'We've passed so many. Some will have to be put down.'

Tye doesn't hear Carla's reply but she sees Lily nod as her mother gives instructions about the wombat in the back.

'Will do,' Lily says. 'And Lena said we can borrow the van if we need to.'

Opal phones, annoyed that Tye hasn't been answering her calls. She's in full flight.

'What's happening? Are you all right? I've been worried sick.'

'I'm fine. We're on our way back to Chancy's.'

'What!' Tye holds out the phone and Opal's voice fills the cab. 'What do you mean? There are fires up there. I've been watching the news, even if you haven't. What's Mum thinking? Put her on, Tye. I want to speak to her.'

'Tell your mother I'm driving,' Nan says quietly, her eyes fixed on the road.

'Will I put it on speaker?'

Nan raises her voice. 'I'm driving!' Then she swings onto the verge, turns off the engine and takes the phone with an exasperated sigh. An uncomfortable conversation ensues.

Tye and Lily get out and check the wombat. Lil says, 'He'll need to be examined. We'll put him in the run for the time being. Mum reckons we can use the shed if there's not enough room in the house for all the creatures. Just till other carers arrive to pick them up.'

Tye leans close. 'Maybe Bailey went to Launceston like Barry told him,' she whispers.

'I said she's fine!' they hear Nan bark. 'We've got a bit going on down here, Opal, if you haven't realised.'

When the girls get back into the ute, Nan's face is red. She's still holding the phone and Opal is yelling, 'I want my daughter back! I can't trust you to be properly responsible for her. Turn that car around and take her to the airport. Do it right now!'

Nan hands Tye the phone and starts the ute.

'Mum, I'm not in any danger. Get off my case,' Tye says quietly.

She ends the call and turns off her phone.

As they unload the wombat at Lakeview, Tye's looking in the direction of the shack.

'I'll go,' she whispers to Lily. There isn't much choice because Carla calls from the wombat run, holding up her phone. 'Lily, can you take over here? Another one's waiting at Merrick.'

'Are you all right, Tye?' Nan asks as they head to Chancy's.

'Sure,' she says, noticing how tired her grandmother looks. It'll be the long hours at the hall, keeping everyone fed and hydrated, reassuring people, and providing what assistance she can to those coordinating the fire effort.

And she must be worried about Pop too, out day after day in the truck. She doesn't need any more worries.

'I'm fine, Nan. Just didn't sleep well last night.'

It's midmorning and Chancy's is deserted: the firefighters are all on the job. Just Lance sitting on the veranda with Myrtle at his feet.

'I need to be at the hall,' Nan says. 'There's still a lot going on. And once Aileen's back I'll be on the second shopping run to Launceston to get food for the firefighters. I'd appreciate it if you kept Lance company for a bit.'

'No problem.' Tye takes her pack and seedling into the house porch.

Outside, Nan is talking to Lance, shaking her head. She frowns for a minute, then walks over to Tye. 'Lance seems a bit under the weather.'

'What's the matter with him?'

'He's old and a bit confused. Nothing for you to worry about.'

'I'll look after him,' Tye says.

'Thanks, love. I'm glad you're back.'

A quick kiss from Nan and the ute is heading up the drive. Tye waves as it disappears. Then she has a few brief words with Lance who tells her he's fine, just worn out with all the excitement.

'Don't work today,' Tye suggests. 'Have a rest.'

She helps him settle onto his bed, Myrtle curled up close by. And when Tye returns with drinks for them both, Lance is sound asleep. *Good, he's set for a few hours.* With a glance over her shoulder she grabs Nan's bike and heads for the shack.

Think positive. Maybe Bailey'll be there. Maybe he didn't leave after all. She knows exactly what she'll to say to him. *Bailey, you've got to go back to Auntie Bev's. If you don't, I'm telling on you.*

She doesn't take any food. Bailey'll come with her, she tells herself. He'll eat at Chancy's. He'll be hungry by now, hungrier than ever.

She rides as fast as she can and by the time she turns down the track she's convinced herself that he'll be there waiting. He has to be. She can almost hear his voice, accusing but full of relief. *Tye, where have you been?* But the shack is deserted. She can tell just by looking at it. Nevertheless, she peers in the window. Nothing's changed. Maybe he's down near the water. She wheels the bike along the path, passing the dinghy. If he's not by the lake perhaps he'll be out looting the empty shacks for food. Her fear turns to annoyance. When she finds that boy she'll let him have it.

Her phone pings. A text from Lily – Find him? Tye texts back, Still looking.

Bailey's nowhere along the shore. Tye gets angrier. *I'll cop it big time from Nan and Pop*, she fumes. *They'll ask what possessed me to leave a boy on his own in the midst of the fires. And they'll be right. What did possess me?*

She throws down the bike and sits to catch her breath. He could be anywhere, she tells herself. But deep down she knows what must have happened. It's as she expected. A sob rises in her chest and once she starts to cry she can't stop.

Now she'll go back and tell Nan – *now* – when it's too late. It should have been days ago, when she first met the boy. Tye waits for the crying to ease, then shakily gets to her feet and pushes the bike back towards the shack. She's almost there when she notices a little saucepan sitting by the door, an old saucepan with a lid. Had it always been there?

She puts down the bike and goes up the broken steps. Lifts the lid. Inside is a note weighted with a stone. *ALL SORTED TYE* – printed in big capital letters with a blunt carpenter's pencil. *THANX FOR HELP.*

She's weak with relief. *Ripped off*, she thinks. *I'll give him 'sorted'!* But at least he's done what he should have, all along – gone back home.

Fourteen

When Tye gets back, Lance's door is open. She peeps in. He's still asleep on his bed and there's no sign of Myrtle. She feels a prickle of anxiety, but tells herself it's okay, Myrtle will be around somewhere.

She heads to her cabin, forgetting it's occupied. There's an extra mattress on the floor and other people's things have joined her own. She sits down outside under the window facing the lake. Turns on her phone. Missed calls and messages pour in from Opal and there's another text from Lily.

All good, Tye replies. He's gone home. Left a note.

She presses SEND. Immediately, a text comes in from Lukas. Hey, RUOK? Just seen footage of burnt World Heritage areas down your way. Ecological disaster. Are they going to wait till all the Gondwanan species are wiped out before they take action? Or is it up to us?

Guess so, Tye responds. Fill you in later.

She's not up to going into the whole story right now. Her mainland friends seem a world away. And Bailey's probably back with Auntie Bev. It's been days. She bets he's at camp, having fun on the beach. She grits her teeth. All that worry for nothing.

Nan returns midafternoon and announces there's a meeting at the hall.

'Another one?'

'The show's not over. Nothing to worry about right now, but the fire service is still concerned. Wants everyone to be kept informed.'

Tye can't remember when she ever felt so tired. She offers to stay home with Lance. 'He's asleep,' she says. 'I think it's all been a bit much for him.' *And for me.*

Nan looks relieved. 'I'll be back as soon as I can.' She peers at her granddaughter closely. 'Opal been on your back?' she asks and Tye nods. 'Mine too. Don't let her get you down.'

Tye makes up her bed in her old spot in the hallway behind the devil curtain. That's what Nan named it. A friend of Opal's printed the fabric when Tye was small and she still likes it. Likes the cubby as well, although it isn't a patch on her beautiful new space. She pulls the curtain closed and tries out her old bunk. Snug as ever, though her feet reach the end board. The ceiling is covered in stars she and Opal stuck on many years ago.

She sighs as she lies down. Thank goodness Bailey's gone home.

Tye drifts off to sleep. Sometime later she's aware of the screen door slamming. That must be Nan, home already. She should have made her grandmother something to eat.

But it's not Nan, and Tye has no idea how long she's slept. She dozes again, waking to the sound of gnawing. Pulling back the curtain she's surprised to find the house almost dark. When she gets up and turns on a light the sound abruptly stops. A trail of felted wool leads into the lounge room, and in the middle of the carpet is a cairn of cubed wombat droppings. Myrtle!

There's no sign of her, but half the couch has been demolished. Myrtle has tunnelled right through the back of it and stuffing is everywhere. The gnawing starts up again and Tye follows the sound into her grandparents' bedroom. The wombat is working on the leg of the bed.

When Tye claps her hands and shouts, Myrtle shakes her head in irritation, turns around and runs full pelt up the hall, before disappearing into the kitchen. Tye hears a crash and then the screen door slamming. There's silence except for someone groaning.

'Lance, are you all right?'

He's on his back, half under the kitchen table. The fridge door is open and there's food and water all over the floor.

'I came looking for her, Opal. I couldn't find her and then I saw . . .' He rolls his head to one side. Not only has Myrtle been in the fridge, she's wreaked havoc in the cupboards, dragging out a bag of flour and knocking packets from the lower shelves.

Lance is all angles and difficult limbs and it takes Tye a while to get him to his feet.

'I'm so sorry, Lena,' he says as he collapses onto a chair. 'I lost track of time. I just lay down for a few minutes and then . . . I'll clean it all up in a jiffy.'

He looks up at Tye in bewilderment. 'Tyenna,' he says, surprised, then puts his head in his hands.

Tye takes in the damage. This is the last thing Nan is going to want to find at the end of the day.

'It's all right, Lance. I'll fix it.'

My fault as much as his, she thinks, as she begins sweeping up flour and noodles. *I was meant to be looking out for him.* She glances at the clock. Eight-thirty.

'I should have been more careful,' Lance mutters. 'How many times has Lena asked me?'

'It's a bad time for everyone,' Tye says. 'The heat, the smoke . . .'

'It's more than that. Your grandmother's getting increasingly short with me. And with good reason.' He shakes his head. 'I thought this might go away but it's getting worse.'

For a split second Tye thinks of confiding in Lance, telling him that she's hardly slept for two days, that she and Lil met this boy and promised to hide him, that he might be in trouble with the police and how, for one terrible night she'd thought he was lost in the fires. Lance would understand. But she sets the urge aside. The old man has his own troubles. Chief of which right now is his beloved wombat. Myrtle has pulled out the cord to the fridge. Lucky she didn't bite through it. Tye plugs it back in, picks up what's left of the vegetables, puts them in the crisper and closes the fridge door.

'My fault, really,' Lance apologises. 'I try to keep an eye on her, but sometimes I forget. There are times I can barely . . .' – he searches for the word – 'function.'

Tye needs to sweep under the table. 'It's okay, Lance. Really it is.' She helps him to his feet. 'We just have to make sure Myrtle doesn't get into any more trouble.'

She turns on the outside light so Lance can see his way back to his room. He lingers at the door, as though uncertain what to do next. 'Much obliged, Tyenna,' he says at last. 'I won't forget your kindness.' Then he hurries away.

Tye has almost restored order to the kitchen by the time Pop arrives home. He looks dead tired, but once he sees the mess, he hangs up his overalls, kicks off his boots and lends a hand. They move on into the lounge room. Tye covers the damaged couch with a blanket.

'Trust Myrtle to go on the rampage at the worst of times,' Pop says. 'Your nan's not going to be pleased. Poor old Lance is a bit past managing her.'

'Why? Is he sick?'

'In a way, I suppose,' Pop replies, stroking his chin. 'Most of the time he's okay, he's the Lance we've always known and loved, constantly on about his fishing, tying flies and making things like that lovely brooch. But as time goes on, I am afraid the memory lapses and confusion will increase. Lance knows that. It's a cruel disease, dementia.'

This new knowledge tightens her chest. Tye feels as if she can't breathe. Does everything have to change? Be lost?

Pop's arm is around her. 'It's sad, chickie, but we just have to enjoy what there is. And with Lance and Myrtle, that's plenty.'

A vehicle pulls up. 'Who's this?' Pop says as he goes to the door.

It's Kelly-Ann, dropping off a couple of exhausted-looking New Zealanders who head straight for their cabin.

Tye waves from the back door. 'How are you going, Kel?'

'End of a big day,' Kelly-Ann replies. 'Another one. Can't do much more in the dark.'

'A cool drink?' Pop offers.

'What's going on here?' Kelly-Ann asks, pointing at the wet kitchen floor. 'Housework?'

'Myrtle,' Tye explains. 'Our wombat. She knocked out the cord to the fridge. Flooded the kitchen.'

Kelly-Ann grins.

'Anyway,' Pop says, 'how are things up in your neck of the woods?'

'We've holding containment lines near Lake Ada. The Hercules air tanker is supporting the ground crews successfully, so far.'

'So the pines are still safe?' Tye wants to know.

'For the moment. Other places aren't going so well. Lot of damage in the Southwest.'

Pop pours four glasses of cordial. 'No ice, courtesy of Myrtle,' he says. 'I'd better go and check up on Lance.' He takes two glasses and goes out.

'You look a bit rocky, Tye,' Kelly-Ann says. 'Rough couple of days, eh?'

'Tell me about it.' Tye thinks of Bailey then puts him out of her mind. It's over now, she tells herself.

Kel sighs and folds her arms on the table. 'What a start to the season!'

'The fire season?'

'That too. But also to my first season as a ranger. Only finished the course in November and straight into the job. Ordeal by fire.' She closes her eyes for a minute then gulps down her drink. 'If this summer ever ends I'll have enough time in lieu for a holiday. I've hardly taken a weekend off since I started.'

'What do you have planned?' Tye asks.

'Site preparation for the pencil pine project plus I'd like to do some seed collecting for the nursery down near Liffey. And bushwalking – that goes with the seed collecting.'

Although Tye's worn out, the thought of going bush and collecting seeds gives her a sudden burst of energy. 'Can anyone come, Kel?'

'Sure. It mightn't be for a while though.'

No good, Tye thinks, *I'll be back in Melbourne.* As if on cue, a text comes in from Lukas. She glances at it. *Read it later,* she thinks.

'Friend of mine from the science club at school,' she tells Kelly-Ann. 'We're organising a climate strike.'

'Good for you. The quicker everyone realises what really matters and we change our ways the better.'

'Listening to the country,' Tye says.

'And looking after it,' Kel adds. 'There's a lot we can do.'

'But where to start?'

'Right here,' says Kelly-Ann. She's about to continue when Nan walks in.

She utters a brief hello and slumps into a chair. 'Things have changed again,' she tells them. 'I've just come from the hall and the news for tomorrow isn't good.'

Tye starts to recount the Myrtle debacle, but Nan shrugs and says, 'That wombat's the least of our worries right now.'

Kelly-Ann rises to go. She gives Tye a hug. 'Sleep well. Can't have our ecowarriors falling over when we need them most.'

Fifteen

Tye wakes long before dawn and sees stars above, the glow-in-the-dark ones she used to love when she was little. Amazing that they're still shining. Then the thought of Bailey arrives, along with a knot in her stomach. She takes a deep breath. He's gone, she tells herself, and probably taken Nan's sleeping bag with him. She didn't think to look yesterday. She checks the time. Not even five o'clock. Decides to nip down and see if it's there before anyone is up.

In the moonlight the rutted track is full of shadows. It's hard to tell how deep the potholes are so Tye gets off the bike and pushes it along. Now and then she sees the lake, gleaming silver through the trees. The air is smoky and warm, and the bush on either side of the track is full of thumpings, rustlings and scrabblings. Perhaps creatures from the burnt-out areas are seeking new homes.

Soon light appears beyond the hills on the far side of the lake and the craggy rim of the plateau appears against a purple sky. She gets back on the bike and rides on, dodging a potoroo that leaps across the track in front of her.

The sun is rising by the time she reaches the shack. The door's locked. She sees her face reflected in the dirty window, cups her hands and peers inside. No sleeping bag. Well, what did she expect? If he'd stolen an outboard motor and a dinghy there'd be nothing to stop him taking a sleeping bag.

Tye picks up Bailey's note and puts it in her pocket. It has her name on it and she wouldn't want anyone else to find it. She's sitting on the steps, looking towards the lake when her eye catches a movement near the tinny. She goes to investigate, creeping close. It's Wanda. What's she doing here? Surely Bailey hadn't abandoned her? Wanda looks up, twitches her ears and her nose, as if to enquire, friend or foe?

A text comes in, then. Hi there Bails, it reads. Haven't heard from you in a while. Still enjoying camp? Looking forward to seeing you soon. Give me call xxx Big B.

Auntie Bev! Why is she texting Bailey? Shouldn't he be with her by now? If not, then where is he? Why has he left Wanda behind? Tye's heart starts to pound. Something bad must have happened.

Stop it, she tells herself. He's on his way home, just hasn't got there yet. Maybe he lost his nerve and is holed up somewhere, gathering his courage before he faces the music.

Her thoughts chase each other in circles, but one keeps returning: there's no way Bailey would leave Wanda behind. Tye needs to talk to Lily. Right now. It's not far to

Lakeview. She sends a quick text to Nan. Gone for an early morning walk – no, that won't go down well. She deletes that and replaces it with, Down by the lake, back soon. Her grandparents might not even be up yet. She won't be long. And if Lily's not awake she'll tap on her window.

It might be her imagination, but is it getting smokier? It's certainly getting hotter. Tye stops and gets off the bike, sniffing the air. It's then that she hears a soft *thump-thump, thump-thump,* behind her. She looks back. It's Wanda. No, she's not dreaming, the little wallaby is definitely following her. Probably hungry. At least if Wanda comes with her to Carla's, she'll get a feed. The wind picks up as Tye heads for the road.

An SES vehicle is parked outside the shed at Lakeview and another vehicle is backed up to the steps, its rear door open. A woman Tye doesn't know is stacking plastic pet containers into the back. Carla, looking slightly worried, is on the deck, talking to a man in uniform. 'It's all go here this morning, Tye. Lily's gone with Brett, but you've come at a good time. I could use an extra pair of hands.'

'Feed time again?' Tye asks.

'Well, no. Clearing the decks before the next lot come in. Pam here is taking most of my charges away and I'm meeting another courier in Merrick soon. Does Lena know you're here?'

Tye nods. Wanda's nibbling grass by the tap near the wombat enclosure. Carla hasn't noticed her yet.

'Things aren't looking too flash,' the SES man says. 'Wind could be a problem. They had a hell of a battle holding the containment lines on Friday. Might get away from them this time.'

'It's still only Watch and Act,' Carla replies. 'No Emergency warnings as yet.'

'Let's hope it stays that way. I'd better get to work. Catch up with Brett next time,' the man says. 'You've got your fire plan in place?'

'All fixed, Phil. Thanks for calling in. We've decided to stay for the time being. Lily has a dance rehearsal tomorrow. If things look like they're getting out of hand up here she can stay in Deloraine.'

As soon as the SES vehicle pulls away, Carla's on the phone. 'Meet you at the hall,' she's saying. 'That's right, the community centre. It's just above the fire station. Park around the back. I won't be long.'

Carla notices Wanda. 'Pam, you didn't leave the door open, did you?'

The woman shakes her head and goes into the house, returning with another crate.

'So where did this joey come from?'

'She followed me,' Tye tells her.

Carla raises her eyebrows. 'Looks pretty nearly big enough to survive on her own, but run inside, will you – there's a bottle on the bench and carrots in the fridge. See if you can put her in the run.'

By the time Tye has fed Wanda and coaxed her in with the wombats, Pam has left and Carla has filled her car with creatures, all safely stowed in boxes and pet crates.

'Hop in, Tye,' she says. 'We have to be quick, while the roads are still open, before anything else happens with the fires.'

As they head down the drive Wanda jumps the fence and hops back to the grass by the tap. Carla sees her in the rear-view mirror and laughs. 'Well, that's the fastest soft release I've ever seen!'

Tye texts Lily. Heard from Bailey's carer. He's not in Launceston. So where is he?

Lily replies: Must be on his way.

He left Wanda.

So? He'd hardly take a joey to town.

Lil's right, Tye thinks. How would he get a lift with a wallaby in tow? For sure he'll arrive today. He must. But what if he doesn't?

She texts again and Lily replies: Class starting talk later

As they head towards Merrick, Tye sees helicopters rising over the hills, water bags slung below. From here they're no bigger than thimbles. The road crosses the familiar plains south of Chancy's. Tye sees this landscape with new eyes – as a brush fire waiting to happen. She tries to put Bailey out of her mind, but he keeps returning.

Carla drives with her elbow out the window, looking towards the smoky hills. 'I wonder where they're filling up?' she says. 'They seem to be holding the fire at bay. With a bit of luck things will settle this evening.'

It's still early but the day is dark. Must be the smoke. What if Bailey's lost out on the plateau, or lying injured or even . . . No, she won't let herself go there. But she can't help it. She sees those maps in her mind, showing swathes of country destroyed by fiery fingers clawing their way over ridges, through hectares of forest. Fires jumping rivers, racing up hills and gullies, charring everything in their path. She texts Lily again: What if he's gone to the bunker?

There's no reply, of course, so Tye imagines one: *Give him time ...*

But we haven't got time, she thinks. Like the scientists say about climate change, it's gone too far. Everything on the brink and now it's tipped over. The planet getting hotter and storms deadlier, icecaps melting, out-of-control fires and floods, rivers and oceans polluted, whole ecosystems destroyed. The world's on fire and Bailey, if he's out there, has no safe place to hide.

Her thoughts race like a wildfire, fanned by fear. Then Carla turns up the road to the hall and Tye pulls herself together. Nan is just arriving. She looks puzzled and annoyed to see Tye.

'Morning, Carla,' she says and turns to her granddaughter. 'Didn't we ask you to let us know where you are at all times?'

'My fault,' says Carla. 'I hijacked her in my hour of need.' As she speaks a van pulls up beside them – the courier.

Someone calls out, 'Lena!' from the hall. 'Wait here,' she says and hurries inside.

Tye helps transfer the animals to the other vehicle. Then Carla nods towards the door. 'You'd better have a word with your nan.'

Tye goes inside. Nan is coming out of the office, phone in one hand and a pile of papers in the other. She almost bowls Tye over. 'Yes, Frank,' she's saying. 'I'll tell him. And if I can't get onto him I'll go and let them out myself. Feed and water them too. Where do you keep your chook feed?' She puts her arm around Tye's shoulder. 'Righto, Frank. If things change you'll be the first to know.' She puts down the phone. 'Now, Tye, I've left Lance by himself so I'd like you to go straight—'

Nan's phone goes off. 'Your mother,' she sighs, ignoring the message. Then somebody else calls to her from the far end of the hall. 'Won't be a second,' she says, handing the papers to Tye. 'Give these to Aileen, will you, love, and tell her to order another gas cylinder. She's in the kitchen.'

When Nan returns she walks Tye smartly to Carla's car. 'I want you to get your things together and tell Lance to pack. No need to panic. It's just a precaution. Pop and I started last night.' She gives Tye a hug and is gone.

Sixteen

The smoke gets heavier as the day passes, thick black smoke that stings Tye's eyes. When she goes over to Lance's room to see how he's getting on, she finds him wiping his watering eyes as he sorts his fishing tackle.

'Lance, it's your clothes you need to pack.'

'Where did you say we were going?' he asks.

'Nowhere. It's just in case.'

Lance shrugs. He points to a handsome fishing rod propped in a corner. 'This is my original cane rod. It must be an antique by now.' He gives a chuckle that turns into an explosive cough.

'That sounds nasty, Lance.'

'It's the heat and the smoke.' He nods towards Myrtle who's burrowing into a heap of clothes on the floor. 'It's affecting her, too. She's not herself today. Hasn't been since she woke up. She's sniffing and snuffling.'

'Maybe she's worn out from all the excavating she did yesterday.'

Lance frowns. 'Look, she's panting.'

It's true. Myrtle doesn't look good. Tye goes off to get some water and a handful of alfalfa sprouts for her, but after taking a sniff, Myrtle refuses both.

'See what I mean?'

Tye nods. 'We'd better keep an eye on her.'

'We'll do that, lass,' the old man agrees.

Nan calls. 'Just updating you,' she says. 'We're still on Watch and Act warning, but the fire is unpredictable. It has split and is now burning back on itself, into the hills northwest of Merrick. We might need to get more preparations underway.' Nan sounds calm until a babble of raised voices in the hall forces her to shout. 'Go to the office, Tye. You'll find our bushfire plan in the desk drawer. There's a checklist—'

'I'll get onto it, Nan.'

'Thanks, love,' her grandmother yells. 'I'll be back as soon as I can.'

Tye springs into action. She finds the plan and checklist, scans what needs to be done. Downpipes first – check them for leaves then block them off. With tennis balls if she can find any, socks full of dirt if she can't. Then fill the gutters with water.

She goes outside and starts searching for a ladder. Everything looks like fuel. Nan and Pop have put the doormats away, already, and the old craypot that they use as a hanging basket on the veranda near Lance's room. But she needs to stash the rest.

Tye drags the picnic tables into the shed. Then she goes to the cabins and takes down the curtains and closes every door and window. She moves to the house and does the same.

'A lot of hoo-ha over nothing,' Lance says, when she returns to take down his blind. 'I'm more concerned with *her*.' Myrtle's looking increasingly sluggish and that worries Tye but she must push on with the fire preparations first. She'll ring Carla for advice when she gets a minute.

Tye fills all the baths and basins and every bucket and jerry can she can find. She returns to the office to check what she needs to collect – bedding, clothes, toiletries, plus a list of things Nan has stapled to the fire plan: *computer hard drive, blue folders from cabinet, photo albums, tools from shed, Opal's box in hall cupboard, passports.* The list goes on.

She hurries about her tasks, trying to stay calm and go about things in an organised way. She collects what she can find, then looks again for the ladder. It's behind the house. Pop must have left it there when he was cleaning out the gutters.

Then she dashes back into Lance's room. He's still fiddling with his fishing gear. 'Lance, your clothes. You need to get them together.'

Tye leaves him to it and heads to her cabin. She collects her things, cramming them into her pack. Pauses a moment to look around her, thinking how she'd hate to lose this haven. But as far as she can tell, the fire's no closer and the warning level hasn't changed. Although now the helicopters are back, filling up at Broadwater.

She takes her pencil pine and puts it in the porch

along with the things she's collected for Nan. Then she turns on the radio in the kitchen. It's roasting in the house. She wipes the sweat from her brow. Still Watch and Act. She needs to fill those gutters.

The *thock thock* of helicopters doesn't let up and soon there are planes on the lake again, those small ones that were there before she left for Studleyvale. They're very fast, swooping low and scooping water. As soon as one takes off the next one comes in.

'Nan should be here by now,' Tye mutters, as she puts the ladder in place near the downpipe. The wind picks up and the aluminium ladder scrapes along the gutter so she puts it back on the ground. She keeps looking up the drive but there's no sign of her grandmother. Then she gets another text from Auntie Bev.

Ring me honey. Haven't heard from you for ages. Everything OK?

Tye thinks of calling back. To say what? That Bailey's on his way? Or that he's missing on the plateau. Lost somewhere on the fireground. She pushes down the thought. What was she doing? The gutters. She needs to get those tennis balls.

She finds them on a shelf in the common room. Her phone sounds again. An unfamiliar number.

'Hello,' Tye says, uncertainly.

'May I speak to Bailey Stokes? He rang me earlier from this number.'

Tye doesn't know what to say.

'Hello? Who am I speaking to?' the voice continues. 'Are you with the Hub Youth Camp?'

'No, I'm . . . no, it's not the . . .' Tye stammers.

'Who is this?' The tone is sharper now. 'I need to know where Bailey is. Can you—'

Tye's heart starts beating hard and she presses END. So, Bailey isn't at home. And he's certainly not at camp. Where *is* he, then?

She's trying to control her rising panic when she hears a vehicle swerve into the drive and pull up near the house. She peeps out the common room window and sees Opal in a sundress, dark glasses and strappy sandals, stepping out of a red hire car. Tye resists the impulse to hide.

As if by instinct Opal spots her daughter immediately. 'Oh babes,' she cries, running into the building. 'You wouldn't believe the trouble I had getting here. Some idiot wouldn't let me through, reckoned I wasn't a local. I told him where to go.'

She holds her daughter close. 'I've been out of my mind with worry, Tye-Tye.'

And for a moment all Tye takes in is the smell of her mother's frangipani perfume. It fills her nostrils and her mind.

Opal steps back. 'Let me look at you,' she says, as the perfume floats between them. Then, seeing Tye's distress, 'What's the matter, hon? What's happened?'

Before Tye has a chance to speak, Nan arrives. Tye sees her frown at the hire car as she heads towards the house. Seconds later Tye hears a siren, loud and close. *Whoop, whoop, whoop.* She jumps back in fright. Opal looks about for the source of the sound. A second alarm follows and Tye feels for her phone. The siren fades and a message comes up: Bushfire Emergency Warning from TFS for Chancy's Bay and surrounding areas. Leave immediately in a northerly direction if path is clear. Check local radio or ...

Tye doesn't finish reading it. She heads outside. Nan must have received the same message, because she's at the porch door with the phone in her hand.

'There you are,' Nan says. 'Don't panic, love. Just gather your things and put them in the car.'

Tye sees Nan's mouth fall open as she spots Opal. 'Tye, get Lance, will you. Grab some blankets and water as well. And the laptop. Just gather everything up and hop in the car, and we'll . . .'

Opal interrupts. 'I'm taking Tye home, Mum.'

'I told you she was fine.'

'Call this fine? The highway's shut. The place is on fire. I could see the smoke from the plane. Is this what you call looking after my daughter?'

'Look who's talking!' Nan yells. 'Off gallivanting around the country, dragging the child from pillar to post. She's always been safe in my care. And you could have at least let me know you were coming.'

'I've been messaging since I landed! Nobody here checks their phones.' Opal stares hard at her mother.

'I'll go and tell Lance to get ready,' Tye says, and slips away.

She wishes she'd helped Lance pack his suitcase. Too late now. They'll just have to stuff things in and go.

As she heads towards the singlemen's quarters she hears her grandmother say, 'Well, Opal, you're here now so we'd better get on with it.' She doesn't hear her mother's reply because a helicopter passes above, its blades beating the air into a maelstrom of noise.

Lance's door is wide open. The heap of clothes is still on the floor but Myrtle and Lance are not there. Must be in the toilet. Tye's hurrying towards the shower block when Brendan's police car pulls in, along with an SES vehicle.

'Just the three of you?' he asks, giving Opal a puzzled look. 'Four, with Lance? We're doorknocking. The fire's taken a run. Don't waste any time. You okay to get going soon?'

Nan nods. 'Everything's under control.'

He gives a thumbs up and jumps back in his car. The two vehicles accelerate away.

Tye checks the toilets and shower cubicles. Lance isn't there. She looks in the office and the common room. There's no sign of him. One after another people are starting to disappear. First Bailey, now Lance. And with all the panic about the fire, and Mum and Nan at each other's throats, everything seems to be spiralling out of control.

Seventeen

Tye hears her mother and grandmother calling for her but she doesn't stop.

'Got to find Lance!' she yells over her shoulder.

She reaches the foreshore, stumbling over the uneven surface in her haste. Smoke hangs over the water and she can't see far but she finds Lance's footprints, heading towards the spot where Pop usually leaves the dinghies. She remembers Pop towed them up to the shed, leaving only a single canoe near the boat ramp. An old one, not used much anymore. Most guests prefer the dinghies with outboard motors to get to their fishing spots as quickly as possible. It's only a dedicated few who are interested in silently paddling a canoe about the lake, and they usually take the swifter, newer models that are racked up behind the common room.

The old canoe is missing. Tye can see drag marks in the mud, and Lance's footprints disappearing into the water. She stares into the smoke and her eyes sting. *Oh Lance, where have you gone?*

A helicopter hovers close overhead, lowering its bucket right in front of her. The sound is deafening. Close up, the bucket looks huge. Water sloshes over the sides as it's hauled skywards. Tye can see how heavy it is. The helicopter swings out wide, struggling with the load, then heads towards the hills directly behind Chancy's.

The wind gets stronger and the smoke clears a little. Tye looks across the water, catches a glimpse of something, a diminutive figure in a tiny craft.

'Lance!' she yells. 'Lance, come back!'

But of course, there's no way he'll hear over the roar of the departing helicopter, and now one of the small planes passes above, heading towards the top end of the lake.

The water's choppy and Lance is making erratic progress. He's paddling towards the Neck. Then the wind grows even stronger and blows him further from the shore. He disappears around the headland.

Only one thing to do, Tye tells herself. Race across the Neck and try and meet him around the other side, catch his attention, call him back, persuade him to beach the canoe and join the evacuation.

It's a long way out to the headland, but not far across the Neck. She should be able to do it. She's young and fast and he's old and slow.

Tye hears her phone. It sounds again and again, but she ignores it. She reaches the Neck in record time and crosses it in a flash. When she turns and runs along the shore on the other side she sees a figure ahead, someone sprinting as if their life depends on it. A kid, a boy. Bailey! What's he doing here? He's a fair way in front and he's running for all he's worth.

Another plane roars overhead.

There's no sign of Lance yet. By the time he comes into view Tye's chest is aching and her eyes streaming from the smoke. She passes an upturned dinghy, an old wooden one with a hole in the bottom. Kids must have been playing in it. There's a stick poking through the hole and a little plastic pinwheel is spinning in the wind, a momentary blur of colour.

Tye slip-slides over rocks in the mud at the water's edge, then reaches a place where the shoreline is smooth wet sand. She has almost caught up with Bailey when the first plane returns, skimming across the surface of the lake and rising again, trailing streams of water. Tye's shocked at the speed.

Soon she and Bailey are running stride for stride. He looks terrified. He too must have seen Lance and realised the danger. The Air Tractors are plying the lake and anyone coming around the headland could be in their path. When the next one appears Bailey shouts and waves his arms. Tye does too.

'Lance!' she yells. 'Lance, come in!'

He can't possibly hear them, but that seems to be exactly what he's trying to do. He's paddling hard, battling to get to the shore. Tye can see he's worn out with the effort. The plane swoops down, skids across the water and takes off with its load. It's nowhere near Lance, but when the wake reaches him the canoe rocks wildly and almost capsizes. Lance drops his paddle and leans out over the side as it bobs away.

'Leave it,' Tye cries. 'Let it go!'

She plunges into the lake. The water balloons her T-shirt and shorts out, and she thinks, *My phone!* but doesn't stop. It's probably already slipped out of her pocket onto the lake bed. Bailey's right behind her. He speeds past and swims with long, efficient strokes.

Lance isn't far from them, but the canoe is starting to drift. Then the wind picks up and blows him further out. To Tye's horror Lance crouches forward and tries to stand.

'Sit down!' she yells.

Her voice carries on the wind and Lance turns around. He spreads his hands, helplessly, then sits, gripping the sides of the canoe.

Bailey treads water for a minute. 'We'll get you,' he calls.

Forging onwards, they swim abreast. Panic propels them, seems to give them superhuman strength. From where they are the old man appears to be drifting right into the path of the Air Tractors.

It seems to take an age to reach him and when they do Lance is doubled over, coughing and gasping for breath. He's on the open water beyond the headland where the wind is strongest. Tye grasps the floating painter and turns the canoe around.

'You push, I'll pull,' she shouts to Bailey.

Tye swims and tugs, swims and tugs, while Bailey heaves from behind, kicking and shoving like mad. And slowly, bit by bit, they manage to bring their cargo back towards the shore.

When they reach the safety of the shallows they pause to get their breath. Lance doesn't look too good. They tow the canoe, letting it glide until they are almost at the narrow part of the Neck. Easier for Lance than struggling along the muddy shoreline on foot.

When they help him out his legs give way. They lower him to the ground and flop onto their bellies for a moment, panting hard. But there's little time to linger. The sky's a dangerous mixture of orange and turbulent grey and the wind is rising. No time to ask Bailey where he's been or what he's doing back here.

'This way!' he yells, over the wind and the roar of planes and the even more sinister sound, like a train gathering speed, of the approaching fire. It bellows closer and closer, till it seems that surely it will engulf them. Choking and sobbing, Tye and Bailey help Lance along. Can they make it back to Chancy's?

Billowing smoke swirls around them, making it impossible to see beyond a few metres ahead. The ground grows firmer under their feet. Tye is startled when a wallaby looms up ahead, then another races past them. She is even more startled to see a copperhead slither by and then a wombat hurtle along, its stumpy legs pumping furiously. Normally shy creatures are rushing by, forgetful of their usual wariness of humans, united in the common desire to reach the water.

The smoke's so thick Tye can't tell which way they're going. She yells to Bailey to stop, and they stumble back the way they've come. Tye catches a glimpse of some bright twirling thing, the pinwheel. A few steps later and they're crouching in the lee of the old dinghy. Bailey scrabbles in the mud and sand, digging like some mad burrowing creature. Tye thinks briefly of Myrtle, then she grasps Bailey's plan and digs as well.

Soon they've made a decent gap and Bailey wriggles in, his top half disappearing beneath the boat. He keeps digging, scooping out mud, wet sand and silt. Then he shoves a big rock towards Tye, before backing out to join her.

Together they heave the boat upward and wedge the rock under one end.

Tye turns to Lance. 'Under here,' she says, 'quick.'

Lance's eyes are open but he doesn't seem to be taking much in. When he doesn't move, she pulls him down onto his hands and knees.

'Steady on, girlie,' he says, almost toppling over.

As Tye guides Lance in under the dinghy she hears thumps and bangs of Bailey heaping mud on the windward side of the boat. She catches sight of him through the hole in the roof. Then Bailey slides back under and heaves the rock away. The dinghy comes down with a thud and then there's total darkness. The three of them lie in the hollow, water seeping around them, Lance in the middle. Despite the heat, they're shivering. Tye pats Lance's hand to reassure him. The old man is wheezing and coughing again. Not good.

Bailey lies still for a minute, panting hard, then yells, 'I'd better go and get help.'

Tye reaches over Lance and grabs Bailey's arm. She doesn't want him heading out into the oncoming fire. 'Stay where you are,' she shouts.

'That's right. Stay put, youngster,' Lance croaks. 'Bushfires are nothing to play around with.' Another burst of coughing follows.

The noise outside is deafening. How did the fire travel so far so fast?

They huddle low, their clothes clammy with lake water, nostrils burning from the smoke. A wave of despair flows over Tye. Nothing will survive this firestorm. The bush and everything she loves will be lost. There'll be no one left in the world but Bailey and Lance and her. She tries to think sensibly: the firefighters will defend Chancy's, water from the lake will quench the fires, rain will come and put it out – it is the Highlands, after all. A shudder runs through her as she imagines Pop and his crew fronting the flames, and Opal and Nan struggling at Chancy's in the face of a fiery holocaust. If they haven't already left. At that thought a tear trickles down her cheek.

Night falls and they no longer hear the sound of planes. The terrible din of the fire continues. Tree limbs crack and thud to the ground. The heat is intense, the confined space claustrophobic.

Lance is no longer gasping and panting, thank goodness. Tye crawls closer and listens. Nothing. Panicked, she puts her hand on his chest, and is relieved to feel it rising and falling with shuddery regularity. He has either passed out or fallen asleep. She hopes it's the latter.

Sometime during that long night the roar of the fire eases. Tye hears sirens and radio voices carried on the wind. Then the wind itself drops. Sensing Bailey is awake, she tries to sit up, and bangs her head.

'Thought you'd gone home, Bailey,' she calls into the murky darkness. 'What happened?'

'Headed for the bunker. Got halfway to the turn-off. I didn't like the look of things. Wanda, neither.'

Bailey's voice echoes in the hollow under the dinghy. 'She took off,' he continues. 'I tried to follow, but got bushed. Too much smoke. Lost me way. Lost Wanda as well.'

Tye hears a snuffling, gulping sound and wonders if Bailey's crying.

'Found shelter,' he says then. 'A few big boulders and an overhang. Nothing to eat, but. Licked dew from the rocks for water. Freezing at night. Just as well I had your sleeping bag or I woulda been a goner.'

He falls silent, then adds, 'Stupid thing to do. That old bunker probably isn't even there anymore.'

'It's there all right but it's a wreck,' Tye tells him. 'And your Auntie Bev rang.'

She hears a startled movement then the clunk of Bailey hitting his head.

'Ow!' he yells, then more quietly, 'What did you tell her?'

Tye doesn't answer. There's a fair bit she and Bailey have to sort out, but not now.

'I found Wanda,' she says after a lengthy pause. 'She came back to your old camp. She's safe.' *Or she was when I last saw her*, Tye thinks.

Bailey raps an excited tattoo on the side of the dinghy. 'Wanda's alive?' he cries. 'Did ya hear that? Alive!'

Lance stirs and begins mumbling in his sleep, '. . . as long as your arm, no word of a lie . . .'

Tye feels him clutching for her hand. He's probably clutching Bailey's as well. 'You're dreaming,' she mutters.

Lance tries to sit up. 'No. I'm wide awake,' he says, battling to speak. 'I saw that walloping great rainbow trout clear as . . .' – he takes a rasping breath – '. . . day.'

'I believe you, mister,' Bailey tells him.

'I can take you straight to the spot, son.' Lance gasps. 'Maybe tomorrow.'

If there is one, Tye thinks.

Lance falls quiet, his breath rattling in his chest.

'We gotta get help for him . . .' Bailey says.

The night seems to go on forever but eventually Tye sees grey dawn through the hole above her head. The pinwheel is gone and a small black leaf wafts through the gap and lands on her chin. It's smooth and shiny as a coin.

Tye and Bailey crawl from their shelter and heave the boat upright. It flips over with a crash. Lance doesn't move.

They gaze about silently. There are smutted embers on the shore and black leaves falling all around them. Smoke still roils through the scrub. Thank goodness the fire hadn't burned right down to the water. There's no sign of the creatures they saw fleeing yesterday. And no sound of birdsong. Just an eerie silence. Then, almost immediately, the sound of a helicopter. So the fire is still burning somewhere. Maybe close by.

'Best make for the road,' Tye says, 'try and catch a fire truck.'

Bailey hesitates. 'You go. I'll stay with the old fella. We oughtn't leave him on his own.'

Tye struggles to her feet and sets off up the track to the road.

Eighteen

It isn't long before a grime-covered fire truck comes rumbling along. Tye waves frantically and the truck pulls up. It's Joe Standish and his crew.

Joe leans out of the cab. 'Young Tye! People are looking for you. Are you all right?'

Tye nods.

'What are you doing out here on your own?'

Tye points towards the track. 'Lance is down there, too, and Bailey. By the lake.'

'Old Lance Armitage, who lives at your nan and pop's place?'

'Yes. He's not too good.'

'And who's Bailey?'

'A boy.' Tye is suddenly so weary she can't continue.

'Okay, we got this,' Joe says. 'We'll check you're okay and call this in. Then we'll hop on down there and pick up the other two.'

He offers her a bottle of water. Tye sips it, her head reeling. Everything has an air of unreality about it. As if in a dream, she hears the fire truck's radio crackle into life.

'Firecomm, this is Merrick three point one, over,' Joe is saying.

Go ahead, Merrick three point one this is Firecomm, over.

'Firecomm, we have found a young girl on the fireground who has survived overnight.' He gives the grid reference, then continues, 'She's conscious, alert and appears well, with no injuries. She has informed us of a boy and elderly man who are in the vicinity. Please have the ambulance meet us at this location and inform the police. Further word back when ambulance arrives.'

Roger that, Merrick three point one, all understood, we will have ambulance and police meet you at that location, over.

'Roger that, Firecomm. Out. Let's go,' Joe says to Tye.

He assigns a crew member to wait at the turn-off, to direct the ambulance. Another hoists Tye into the truck. Joe reverses and bumps down the ragged track to the water. Tye points along the foreshore to where Bailey's supporting Lance beside the dinghy.

'Is that the kid?' Joe asks.

Tye nods.

'Where'd he spring from? Not from round here, is he?'

Tye doesn't answer. She gulps the water. She hadn't realised she was so thirsty.

Two members of the crew attend to Lance and Bailey, both of whom are the worse for wear.

'You're Reg Stokes' grandson, aren't you?' Tye hears one of the fireys ask. 'I'd know that face anywhere. The beaky nose, the freckles. Skinny, too, like your pop.'

'Uncle,' Bailey mutters. 'Great-uncle.'

Joe Standish turns to Tye. 'You just rest while I ring the Lodge. Your nan's crazy with worry.'

'Is Chancy's . . .' Tye begins. She's almost too scared to ask about it, and whether Opal and Nan got away safely. 'They're still there? They didn't evacuate? And the Lodge is okay?'

'The short answers are yes, no, yes,' Joe says. 'Though she might have a thing or two to say to you kids, skylarking about in the middle of a fire.'

Bailey looks apprehensive but Tye is full of relief. They've survived, Chancy's Lodge is still standing, and even if Nan and Opal both blow their tops at her, everyone's safe.

'Don't worry,' she tells Bailey. 'Things will work out somehow.'

She listens as Joe makes the call, hears Nan's muffled cry and Opal shouting, 'What? What?'

The call is brief.

Then it's Tye's turn to worry. Just how is she to explain to Nan why she kept Bailey a secret? Why she didn't ask Nan what to do? What if Opal blames Nan for not noticing what was going on and Tye is hauled back to Melbourne on the next plane?

'Joe,' Tye says tentatively, 'do you think I could go home now?'

Joe looks at her speculatively. 'By rights we should wait till the ambulance gets here,' he says. 'That's what we've radioed in.'

'But Mum . . . Nan . . .' She can't go on.

Joe scratches his chin. 'Okay. Will do. But these two stay right here. The old fellow needs hospital care, and the police'll take care of the kid. Get him back home. I'll leave two of the crew with them.'

Tye glances anxiously in Bailey's direction, but he seems not to have heard Joe's remark about the police, thank goodness.

She feels a pang as the trio are separated. She hopes Bailey won't be in trouble. 'See you soon,' she tells him and Lance. Bailey is pale and silent, Lance coughs and nods.

Then the fire crew must get cracking, Joe tells Tye. 'The fires are by no means under control, although, provisionally, this area is no longer under threat.'

As far back from the road as she can make out, all Tye can see is a mute forest of tall, blackened poles – remnants of the once flourishing bushland. The air has an ashy taste. She averts her eyes from the charred remains of animals on the roadside and tries not to think about the last hours and minutes of these doomed creatures' lives.

At the Chancy's turn-off Tye gasps. The once familiar surroundings are almost unrecognisable. The fire has burned right to the backyards of dwellings. There's a strange smell in the air, soot and dampness mixed with an odd, unrecognisable odour that has her wrinkling her nose.

'Foam,' Joe says. 'Rotten stuff but it does the job. We certainly spread it around! Fences, houses and shacks, woodpiles, cars, the lot. And you see, it worked. Hey, remind your grandma to empty her tanks. The water'll be contaminated.'

Just as well I filled the bath and all those buckets and jerry cans, Tye thinks.

Chancy's Lodge slides into view then. Beyond, a glimpse of the lake, winking in the sunlight.

'Glad to see the old place still standing?' Joe says.

Tye nods. She gazes about her, trying to take the scene in. It's the same, but different in a way she can't put into words. Fire changes everything.

Two dishevelled figures are standing outside the office, their arms around each other. The sight gives her a shock. For a moment she doesn't recognise them. Then she tugs on the doorhandle as the fire truck rolls to a stop.

'Mum! Mum! Nan!' she calls, and both come running. They throw their arms around her, squeezing her so hard she can barely breathe.

Opal is crying like a small child. She smooths Tye's hair over and over. Then holds her at arms' length, examining her daughter from every angle. 'Are you hurt?' she asks, again and again. 'I can't believe you're okay,' she keeps repeating, with a mixture of laughter and tears.

Nan is the first to recover. 'Thank you so much for bringing Tye home,' she says to Joe. 'Where did you find her?'

'By the lake,' Joe says. 'And she might have a few things to tell you, I'm thinking.'

'Lance?' Nan's voice is sharp with anxiety.

'Oh, he'll be okay. Few more years in him yet. Pretty knocked about by the heat and smoke, but. An ambulance is coming to pick him up. Won't be long. They'll check him out at the hospital.'

Then the fireys are on their way, another full day's firefighting ahead.

Nan takes Tye's arm and leads her inside. 'First things first,' she says. 'Breakfast. *Then* talk.'

Tye stumbles as she steps into the porch. The previous day's adventure is finally catching up with her. She shakes her head at the proffered oatmeal and toast her mother and grandmother fall over each other to prepare, and gulps down two large mugs of sweet tea instead. Her stomach is rumbling but it's not ready for food yet. She's waiting for the tirade to begin, waiting for the two women to start blaming each other for everything. But they don't.

'Is Pop out with his crew?' Tye finally asks, avoiding the subject of Bailey for the moment.

'He didn't come home till the wee small hours, and there wasn't a great deal of sleep happening after that, I can tell you,' Nan says. 'We forced him to take a nap, but he was up and out at sparrow fart.' And she and Opal smile at each other.

Tye is surprised, not that her conscientious grandfather left at dawn to fight more fires, having been up most of the night, but at the novel sense of harmony that seems to exist between the two hovering women.

'How was it here?' she asks.

'Pretty torrid,' Nan replies, 'especially after you and Lance disappeared. My impulse was to go after you but we didn't get a chance. The fire was on us before we knew it. Nobody expected it to move so fast. I rang and rang, but you didn't answer your phone. Then I barely had time to call the police and report you both missing.'

The three of us, you mean, Tye adds silently.

Nan blows her nose several times in rapid succession, blinking back tears.

'So we just had to do what was needed and hope for the best.'

'I was frantic,' Opal says, 'but Mum kept her cool. She was awesome.'

'Your mum wasn't too bad herself,' Nan says, nodding in Opal's direction. 'She was the one who got the fire pump going. And she's pretty handy with a beater, I can tell you.'

'You're no slouch either, for an old girl,' Opal says, and the two of them laugh.

Tye can't believe her ears, her mother and grandmother agreeing with each other. Giving each other compliments.

'It was touch and go there for a while,' Nan continues, 'but we did what we could, and the fireys were brilliant. They're the real heroes.'

'That reminds me,' Tye interrupts. 'Joe said something about emptying the tanks.'

'We're onto it,' Opal says, sounding so much like Nan that Tye is suddenly reminded – yes, they are mother and daughter, like her and Opal, plenty of differences, but when push comes to shove, they make a good team.

Tye is at last induced to nibble a slice of toast. The first buzz of happiness is being replaced by the jittery knowledge that sooner or later she's going to have to do a lot of explaining. But first . . .

'What about the Lance situation?' Nan asks quietly. 'What happened there?'

'Maybe the smoke and all the noise upset him,' Tye replies. 'He took the canoe and set off round the point. I went after him. Found him on the other side of the Neck. Pulled him back to shore.'

There's a sharp intake of breath from the two women.

'But the planes,' Opal says, covering her face with her hands.

'That's what we were worried about,' Tye tells them. 'Lance could have been killed.'

'We? Who's *we*? Joe mentioned there were three of you.'

'That's right,' Tye says, then stops. This is it, she realises, the place where she comes clean. Where the true story comes out. 'Bailey was with me. We did it together, Bailey and me. We got Lance out of harm's way and back to the shore. We hid under a dinghy.'

'Who is this Bailey?' Nan's voice is quiet, measured. 'How did he come to be at the lake?'

'Bailey Stokes. He ran away. He didn't want anyone to know he was here. He thought they'd put him in Barton Hall. I'm sorry, Nan, I should have told you but I promised him I wouldn't. I took him food.'

'Well, that solves the mystery of the diminishing pantry stores, at least,' Nan says. 'And where is he now? Not out roaming around in the fire areas, surely?'

'He's with Lance, waiting for the ambulance.'

Tye hangs her head.

'Bailey didn't know his uncle had died – he was waiting for him. And then the fires came and everything. Please don't let Bailey get into trouble, Nan. If he hadn't been there, I couldn't ever have rescued Lance on my own.'

'I don't know what to say,' Nan says. 'I thought you had more sense than this, Tye.'

Curiously, it's Opal who seems to understand.

'She's just a kid, Mum, and she's had a lot on her plate lately, what with me being tied up with the film, and you and Dad flat out with all this bushfire carry-on.'

'When did you first meet this boy?' Nan asks.

'I don't know,' Tye says. All the days seem to have jumbled together. 'I think it was the day after I arrived.'

'And you kept him secret all that time? You could have spoken to Pop or me.'

'I wanted to,' Tye tells them. 'But when the fires started and Bailey disappeared it all got complicated. I was so scared I couldn't think straight.'

Tye feels Nan's long, hard gaze on her. She waits for her grandmother to tell her she's a disappointment, that she's acted deceitfully and irresponsibly. For a while, no one speaks. Then Nan picks up the phone.

'Who are you calling?' Tye asks.

'Brendan. We'll get him to pick up Bailey, and then we'll decide what needs to happen. Getting in touch with his people is the first priority, I imagine.'

'Joe's already taken care of that,' Tye says. 'And Bailey hasn't got any people. Only Auntie Bev and she's not his real auntie. He lives in a group home.'

Nan looks at Tye doubtfully. 'I think I'll ring Brendan anyway.' She goes outside to make the call.

Police! Tye feels alarmed. Brendan's a nice guy, but he's still a policeman. Will he lock Bailey up?

Nan returns looking thoughtful. 'Poor mite,' she says. 'That Bailey's probably the last of a long line of Stokeses round these parts. There were mobs of them here, one time.' She wipes her brow and Tye sees how tired she looks. 'Maybe I should try and contact his carer,' she says. 'But first things first. We've a bit of cleaning up to do here.'

'Oh, by the way,' Opal says, 'that boy you go to the science club with rang here. Said you weren't answering your mobile.'

'Lukas,' Tye says.

'That's him. We were too flat out to chat, as you can imagine.'

'I'll call him back,' Tye says. Then a sudden thought comes to her. 'My pencil pine – what happened to it?'

She pictures the seedling destroyed by the tremendous heat of the fire – shrivelled to a dead stick.

'Opal wrapped it in a wet towel and put it in the bathroom, first thing,' Nan replies.

Tye heaves a sigh of relief. 'Thanks, Mum. I was afraid the fire would get it, or that Myrtle might nibble bits off it.'

'We put Myrtle in Lance's room to keep her safe,' Nan says. 'I guess we'd better go and see what damage she's done.'

When they push open the door to Lance's room, the familiar bulk of Myrtle is visible at the foot of the bed.

'Oh, here you are!' Tye exclaims. She strides across the room. Then stops. There is something unnaturally still about the sleeping Myrtle. She gently nudges Myrtle with her foot then bends to stroke her head.

Myrtle does not respond. She won't respond ever again.

Nineteen

There's a flat spot not far from Tye's cabin that has a view out over the Neck. Tye takes the mattock from the shed and starts digging. The ground is rock hard and in half an hour she hasn't made much progress. She's leaning against a tree, getting her breath, when Lily appears in a lilac dress, low-key compared with most of her frocks. She has a circlet of jasmine on her curly hair and a carton in her arms.

'So where's Bailey?'

'Brendan took him back to Launceston.'

Lily raises her eyebrows. 'And what did your nan have to say?'

'She talked to his carer. Talked again this morning.'

'But what did she say *to you*?'

Tye picks up the mattock. Her grandparents haven't said much at all. Neither has Opal for that matter. Maybe she'll get hauled over the coals later. Maybe not.

'They were just relieved we were safe.'

'You're lucky is all I can say. Mum and Dad are

threatening to ground me for life. They said I should have told them about Bailey straight away.' Lily examines the spot where Tye's digging. 'I'll get some water. Soften the ground.'

Tye sees tangly vines of jasmine sprouting from Lil's carton. Also sprigs of heath and bottlebrush, and a bunch of blue gum leaves. Underneath, a little solar panel, a string of fairy lights and a coil of fine wire.

Lily returns carrying two full buckets. She empties them into Myrtle's grave. 'We'd better let it soak a while.'

She takes the jasmine circlet off her hair and begins threading heath through it.

'Where did you get the flowers?' Tye asks.

'From home. Lucky the fire didn't touch Lakeview.' She holds up the circlet and looks at it critically. 'A wreath or the beginnings of one. Do you think we should wear them or hang them on the trees?' She gives a half smile. 'You probably think it's silly, that I'm making a big performance—'

'It's a great idea, Lil. Myrtle's pretty important. She's part of Chancy's.' Tye falls silent. For a moment the two girls watch the water soak into the dry earth, then Tye starts digging again, swinging the mattock over her head, putting her back into it. It's good to be working; it eases her sadness. She stops to kick a big clod of dirt off the blade. 'What do you reckon?' she asks, puffing. 'Deep enough?'

'Keep going,' Lily says. 'You're not even halfway there.'

Tye takes the buckets and goes back for more water.

When she returns, Lily has finished half a dozen wreaths and is tying them to the trees.

'They look pretty cool,' Tye says.

'I want to make it as special as possible,' Lil replies. 'Myrtle's important to me as well. You know Mum had her as a pinkie before Lance brought her to Chancy's. I've known her since *I* was a pinkie.'

Tye grins at her friend. 'Nan says she was twenty-five. Pretty old for a wombat, isn't it?'

'Yep. She had a good life though.'

Lily pulls a notebook from the bottom of the carton. 'I'm putting Lance down for the eulogy. He knew her best. He should be the one to do it. How is he, by the way?'

'All right. He wasn't badly hurt. Just needed to rest a bit. He'll be here later.'

Tye pours more water into the hole while Lily strings up the fairy lights.

'They don't show much in the daytime,' Lil says as she wires them in place. 'But they'll look great tonight. And wombats are mostly nocturnal.'

By the time they've finished, the area is looking festive. Not that there's much to celebrate, Tye knows. Heaps of the Highlands burnt to a frizzle and the fires still burning, but at least no one's been seriously injured, except for all the bush animals. Deaths like Myrtle's are just part of the natural order of things.

When it's time to move Myrtle to her final resting place the girls half drag, half carry the wombat, slung in a folded sheet between them.

'She weighs a ton,' Lily pants.

They make their way slowly to the grave site, resting every few steps and by the time they arrive, they're laughing, despite the situation. Then Tye finds herself suddenly overwhelmed by tears. Lily waits till Tye's tears turn to sniffs, then covers Myrtle with the sheet, tucking it under her. 'Hospital corners, like Mum does,' she says. She drapes her arm around Tye's shoulder as they walk back to her bike, which is leaning against the laundry wall.

'I'm going home to get the pièce de résistance,' she says. 'Won't be long.'

'The what?' Tye asks, but Lily's already pedalling away.

Nan and Opal are busy making sandwiches. Nan asks Tye to get a couple of fold-up tables from the shed and set them up for Myrtle's farewell. That's what she calls it.

When Tye returns she finds her grandmother arranging dozens of carrot sticks on plates.

'It won't be a big spread,' Nan says. 'Just a few sandwiches and as many of these as you feel like cutting up.' She nods at a bucket behind the door. 'A farmer up the coast donated them, got Brett to deliver a load to the hall this morning. They won't miss a few.'

Much of the smoke has cleared by evening and a bushfire moon rises in the east. Lily's lights glitter like stars and Lance is wearing a suit for the occasion. It's rumpled and far too big, but he's hooked one of his best fishing flies in the lapel and looks pleased with himself.

When Lily arrives with her parents, Nan and Carla walk with Lance, one either side of him. A couple of the New Zealanders join them, the firefighters who are staying in Tye's cabin.

'The suit hasn't had an airing for quite a while,' Lance says. 'Found some of the old money in the pocket; a shilling and two sixpences. And guess what was in the sleeve – a little bat!'

'Where is it now?' Carla asks.

'In the wardrobe. Quite a cosy home for the little tyke.'

Tye walks ahead with Pop, who's carrying a pair of fold-up chairs. 'One for the old fellow,' he says, 'and one for me. Getting weary, I am.' He winks at her. 'Reckon this might be my last season on the truck. Maybe I'll move to Operations next year. Have a go at wrangling the phones rather than hauling hoses about.'

'Give them to me, Dad,' Opal says, taking the chairs and hurrying on to catch up with Lily. Tye hears bits of their conversation. '. . . and then in the last scene they find her in the rainforest. Great script. And the dancing was like Bollywood.'

'I'd love to be in a movie like that,' Lily says.

Lance takes a hanky from his top pocket and dabs his eyes when he sees the mound encircled by stones and Lily's big bunch of wildflowers in the middle.

'It won't be the same without her,' he says, collapsing into a chair. He rests for a while then stands and clears his throat. 'Here's to good friends and good fishing.

And to Myrtle, a treasured companion and dear friend. She was one in a million, so much more than a humble wombat.'

'She wasn't that humble,' Nan says. 'Don't forget she went straight through the back of my couch. And that was just one of her crimes!'

A smattering of laughter from the group.

'Myrtle caused a fair bit of damage over the years,' Pop admits, 'but she brought us together as well.'

'Like the fire,' Opal says, looking at her mother.

Lance clears his throat again. 'I'd like to thank young Tyenna and the lad, wherever he is.' He looks around the gathering. 'Apparently I got into a spot of bother in the shallows a couple of days back and they came to my aid.'

In the shallows! More like deep water, but Tye doesn't correct him.

'When that boy shows up, I'm going to teach him how to *really* fish. It's the least I can do to thank him.'

Carla hands around a photo of Myrtle as a pinkie. 'There never was a sweeter child,' she says.

Tye is surprised to see Nan's eyes fill with tears. She's surprised by her own tears as well. It's the second time today. She blinks them back and glances around. For a moment everyone looks tired and grey and Tye realises she's crying for more than just a single wombat. There's the scorched country and the thousands of creatures who have lost their lives. And many fires are still burning. They might burn for months. The future is full of uncertainty, not just her own but everyone's.

Then Nan dries her eyes and announces that it's time for the refreshments. Lily takes off at a run, returning with a platter covered by a sequined cloth.

When everyone has a cup of tea in one hand and a sandwich in the other, Lily nods to her dad. Brett picks up a couple of sticks and does a slow drum roll on the end of the table.

'Ta daaa!' Lily unveils her creation to cries of delight and a round of applause. It's a miniature wombat and it appears to be grazing on a bed of parsley. The proportions are perfect and it's bright orange. 'Hand carved,' she says, 'from the thick end of a gigantic carrot!'

'A work of art,' Lance mumbles and he dabs at his eyes once more. 'It's the sort of thing Myrtle would appreciate.'

Everybody laughs.

'Photo,' Lily says. She hands her phone to Tye. 'Come on, everyone, get in the picture.'

'I can't believe that wombat,' Opal remarks. 'Where on earth did you find a carrot that big?'

'Horse carrots,' Brett tells her. 'For the wildlife. Our Kiwi friends'll be airlifting them in, tomorrow.'

'You're going to drop carrots from a helicopter?' Tye asks one of the firefighters.

'As many as we can carry.'

Tye takes a snap with the wombat creation in the centre. Then she does a close-up of the bouquet on Myrtle's grave. 'Okay if I use your phone to send a pic to Lukas, Lil?' she asks.

Lily nods. Tye texts: Still some wildflowers about. Not everything got burnt.

Then she sends a photo of the gathering to Jas. Here we all are at Myrtle's goodbye. Ace wombat. Mum says hi.

Footsteps approach. 'Anyone around?' a voice calls, and Kelly-Ann emerges from the darkness, takes in the fairy lights and grins. 'What's this? A party?'

'Funeral,' Nan tells her. 'We lost our wombat.'

'Sorry to hear that. I was wondering how you all fared when that fire took a run.'

'Myrtle's the only casualty,' Pop says. 'Well, the only one from Chancy's Lodge. It could have been worse.'

'How are things?' Kel asks Tye. 'Tough time, eh?'

'Tougher for the pines,' Tye replies. 'Any idea how many have been lost?'

'Too early to tell. Maybe there won't be as many as we feared, not this year anyway. When did you get back?'

'I didn't evacuate.'

'What? No time?'

'Something like that,' Tye says. 'We had a bit of drama.'

Kel seems to be waiting for her to explain, but Tye says nothing more.

'How's your seedling going?' Kel asks.

'Pretty good. It almost had a setback but I think it's fine. How big should it be before I plant it out?'

'It's ready now. Talking about seedlings, we're going ahead with this year's planting soon, fires and weather permitting. Are you still keen?'

'You bet.'

'Great. It'll be in the next few weeks.'

'Oh, but I can't.'

'Going back to the mainland?'

'Guess so.'

'Another time, maybe,' Kel says. 'W're getting a team of volunteers in place. We might base ourselves at Chancy's.' Then her mouth drops open at the sight of the carrot wombat. 'What's this?' she cries, heading towards it.

Tye sees her mother standing apart from everyone else. Opal's holding a wreath and looking in Tye's direction. She goes over to Opal. 'How did the film go, Mum? You didn't tell me.'

'I had two screen tests on location and it was looking good but then I had to leave. It doesn't matter, Tye. There'll be other opportunities.'

'Mum, there's something I want to ask you.' Tye takes Opal's hand and leads her away from the gathering. 'It's something I've been thinking about for a while.'

That isn't strictly true but now the idea has arrived it feels as though it's always been there, and only now is she ready to admit it.

'School goes back next week,' she begins.

'I know,' Opal says, raising her voice. 'You think I don't keep track of these things, but I do!' She looks over her shoulder towards Nan, then gives Tye an apologetic smile. 'Sorry, hon. Didn't mean to flare up.' She squeezes Tye's hand and waits for her to continue.

'Well, I was wondering . . .'

There must be an easy way to say this – a soft way, a quiet way. Or should she just blurt it out, like Opal would, or Lily for that matter. Tye decides it's better to be direct and tries again. 'I'm wondering how you'd feel if . . .'

Opal turns and gives her a steady look. 'You want to stay, don't you?'

They are almost eye to eye. 'You've grown,' Opal says. 'Look at you.'

'Yep, I think I have.' Tye holds her mother's gaze. 'And I do want to stay here, Mum. I could go to school with Lily on the bus. You and Jas could live here too. There's plenty of room.'

Opal's quiet for a long time, then she gives Tye a hug and says that she'll think about it, talk it over with Nan and Pop, and with Jas.

'Jas would love it here. I know she would,' Tye says.

'Maybe for a holiday,' Opal suggests. 'But Jas's life is in Melbourne and mine . . .' She looks at her daughter. 'But what matters is that *you* love it here. Right?'

Tye nods and gazes towards the tables. Lily's fairy lights seem to be getting brighter, or is it the moon shining through the trees?

Twenty

Tye hasn't found it at all difficult to fit into her new life. She loves seeing Pop every day and Nan is teaching her to cook some pretty awesome stuff. She does miss gelato though and sushi and Thai. There's so many different types of food in Melbourne, and all of it mouth-wateringly brilliant.

But it's great meeting Lily on the school bus each morning and catching up as they trundle down to the District High, though she misses Jas dropping her off at the school gate on her way to work in the city. They used to have such great conversations. But FaceTime is a pretty good substitute, and Opal's been calling regularly, between acting gigs. Tye smiles every time she takes out the cool new phone her mother sent her.

At first she finds it strange just how small the school is, but she likes the way kids of all ages do stuff together – it's not just those in the same year-group hanging out with each other; that wouldn't work in Bothwell because there aren't enough students.

In the bushfire recovery program, everyone is encouraged to talk about their experiences and even kids as young as six and seven are listened to with respect. Everyone has a story worth telling, Heather Massey says. She's the Year Eight teacher who runs the program. She's also the school counsellor. Some of the stories are pretty scary. Some quite funny. One little kid shook the whole time he was speaking and when he finished, one of the senior students, a big motherly girl, gave him a hug and said, 'You did very well, Stanley. You're so brave.' Tye thinks so, too.

Sharing stories didn't take away the memory of the terrifying night under the dinghy with Lance and Bailey, but it made Tye know she was not alone. They had all been through the fire, in their own particular way. That was what united them.

Now it's spring. The end of the school holidays. Months have passed since the fires. Tender green leaf-whorls are circling burnt trunks, and ground that was once black is covered with bright new growth.

Tye looks out the car window as they head to Launceston. Most of the wattles have gone but the eucalypts are coming back. Not the cider gums, though. They stand like stark scarecrows, witness to the devastation she'd observed, the bare ground and the scorched bush where Carla and others had set up feeding stations. Thousands of animals were lost in the summer fires and those who survived would have starved afterwards without that food.

Lily and Bailey are chatting in the back seat. Lily's offered to do Bailey's chart and Tye's surprised how keen he seems. Especially about auspicious signs.

'Astrology's not just about lucky days,' Lily is saying. 'It's much more than that. I'll explain it all once I've downloaded it.'

'I don't need the whole year,' Bailey tells her. 'Just the fishing season.'

Tye sees Nan glance in the rear-view mirror and frown. 'Bailey, next time you visit, you and Lance are not to go fishing without another responsible person. I insist. Lance might think he's invincible but if he fell in the lake he might not make it to shore.'

'It's okay, Bailey,' Tye assures him, 'three can fit in the canoe.'

'Then me and Lance would have to split it three ways.'

'Split what?' Nan asks.

'The prize money, of course,' Tye says, 'for the tagged fish. Ten thousand dollars. Right, Bailey?'

'And you'll want a cut as well, I suppose.' Bailey looks sideways at Lily. 'That's if you get the day right.'

Lily shakes her head. 'Why do you need all that money anyway?'

'For my licence.'

Lily bursts out laughing. 'But you're not old enough to drive!'

'Not a car, a helicopter. Auntie Bev looked it up. The training costs a lot.'

'That's really thinking ahead,' Nan says.

'Do you want Lance's chart as well?' Lily asks. 'If he can remember his birthday.'

Bailey nods. 'Good idea. Everyone'll be after those trout. I'm lucky to have Lance as my fishing partner. He won the Worlds, you know. Twice.'

Lily groans. 'Tell us something we don't know.'

Tye looks back out the window and watches the passing country. It's taking time, but the bush is starting to recover and the creatures are coming back. She remembers the silence straight after the fires and how long it took to hear the birds again. Except for the crows. They returned almost immediately, feasting on carrion. It was ages before she heard a frog croak.

Time's a funny thing, it seems to Tye. It feels like aeons ago that the crews were battling the fires and then mopping up afterwards. Pop and Kay and others had been on high alert for months. But in another way it feels as if the fires ended yesterday.

Change is rushing forward at a dramatic rate. The Great Acceleration, Lukas reminds Tye, in a text, we're in the Pyrocene now. The Earth hurtling into a new geological epoch. So much change in just a few decades – time speeding up. It's certainly sped up for Tye and whirled her into a brand-new life, where working for the environment has become her first priority.

It's only a year since Greta Thunberg first protested outside the Swedish parliament, and now teenagers the world over are organising school climate strikes.

Hope lies only in action – that's the Swedish girl's message. Tye agrees. She's super pleased to be helping Mrs Massey with next term's follow-up to the bushfire recovery program – a series of talks and workshops called 'Looking after the Land, Looking after Ourselves and Each Other.'

A group of interested students met in the holidays with their teacher to brainstorm topics and possible speakers. TFS and Parks and Wildlife Service people, wildlife carers, farmers, scientists, doctors, police, community nurses, artists and musicians, climate activists, even the local Member of Parliament – all had been suggested.

'We have enough for a ten-year program,' Mrs Massey comments as she reads out the long list scrawled on the whiteboard. 'But there are two others I'd like to invite.'

She adds *fire ecologist* and *Indigenous cultural burn practitioner*.

'We need to understand more about fire,' she says. 'I know we all think of fire as dangerous, and it is. But used carefully it can also be a valuable tool.'

Tye thinks of how the old man, Ted, had talked about the way the Big River people had used fire to create pasture for the wallabies, and to keep the undergrowth down.

'Last week I witnessed what I'd call a healing fire,' Mrs Massey goes on. 'One I'd really like you all to see.'

'Was that at Bella Downs in the Midlands?' Riley Forth asks.

'It was. Not much goes unnoticed in these parts, I see.'

Riley grins at the others. His mother runs the post office so he's always in the know.

'A First Nations man from the mainland, Walter Jessup, came down to run it,' Mrs Massey continues. 'He was taught by traditional people and now he travels about, showing farmers how to use fire in a good way, to keep the land healthy. He's even written a book about it.'

There's a buzz of conversation. When it quietens, Mrs Massey starts to describe the workshop. 'Walt asked us to pick up dead branches first, then he lit the grass and we watched the fire creep slowly along the ground, swallowing the leaf litter and working its way under the trees, then—'

'Whoosh!' Jen Tully shouts and everyone laughs.

'Well, you're both right and wrong,' Mrs Massey says. 'Now and then a bush'd flare up, but then it'd settle. And there was plenty of time for the creatures to get out of the way. It was very peaceful, following that careful fire and watching the smoke drift gently into the trees. Walt told us that this sort of fire keeps country happy.'

Mrs Massey turns to the whiteboard and adds a big tick. 'And the good news is he's agreed to come to school!'

Tye's thinking all this over as they travel along. There'll also be a propagating workshop. People from the nursery who'd sprouted Tye's seedling will bring kits for all the students. Seeds too, and information about local vegetation. And Tye's glad that Glenn Walden is coming. He's Kelly-Ann's friend, the one who's running the pencil pine project.

Tye helped out three weekends in a row back at the end of summer. She planted hundreds of seedlings. But her own little tree is still sitting outside her cabin. She's got used to seeing it there and admires it every morning.

They reach Poatina. Lily's picking up a sewing machine from a friend of her mum's.

'Point the way, Lil,' Nan says.

They stop outside the house.

'Want a hand?' Bailey offers.

Nan watches them go inside. 'It's good Carter's been moved on,' she remarks. 'It's made all the difference to Bailey.'

Tye turns to her grandmother. 'I just want to say thanks, Nan.'

'What for?'

'Everything. When I met Bailey I told him you and Pop would help him out and you have, big time.'

'Well, Bev had a lot to do with it too. She wasn't about to let a good kid like that go down the tube. Anyway it's worked to our mutual benefit: Bev brings the kids to Chancy's for holidays, Bailey and Lance get to go fishing and Bev and I spend time together. She's one in a million, that woman.'

'So are you,' Tye says, suddenly shy.

'You're pretty special yourself, you know that, don't you?' Nan replies.

When they turn into Bailey's street in Kings Meadows, Auntie Bev's in the garden with a little girl who can't be more than three.

'Thanks heaps for letting me come and stay, Mrs Z,'

Bailey says he grabs his bag and jumps out onto the pavement.

'Always a pleasure to have you with us, young man,' Nan replies.

'Look after Wanda for me, Lil.'

'No choice,' Lily replies. 'I don't know where she goes at night but she's on the deck each morning, waiting for breakfast.'

Nan puts down the window and leans out. 'I'll call in later in the week, Bev. Can't stop right now. These girls have a shopping list as long as your arm.'

Twenty-one

The start of Term Four couldn't be better. Walter Jessup visits on Wednesday and the school is abuzz for the rest of the week. Now it's the weekend and Tye finds herself heading west with Kelly-Ann. She holds the seedling carefully between her feet.

'Seems healthy enough,' Kel says as they bump along the corrugated road. 'You've been looking after it well.'

'I reckon it's grown,' Tye says.

Kelly-Ann laughs. 'You could have planted it when we did the others, you know.'

'It was too soon,' Tye tells her. 'For me, I mean.'

They pass a dam wall and the road gets rougher. Soon it's no more than a deeply rutted track.

'It wasn't this bad last time, Kels.'

'Had some rain since then. Hold on.'

Tye puts the pencil pine on her lap as Kelly-Ann changes gear, trying to avoid a washout. She slows down, almost to walking pace, and it's afternoon by the time they arrive at the end of the track.

In the distance Tye sees a familiar-looking grove of mature pencil pines; it's where they camped when the planting crew was here. The ridge beyond is partly lost in cloud.

Kelly-Ann gets tools out of the back. Puts hammer and pliers in Tye's pack then picks up the rest of the gear – mattock, poles and mesh for the tree guard.

'We want to give this little baby every chance it can get. A couple of bites from a passing marsupial and that could be the end of it.'

The path to the research site goes through the grove then winds its way across marshy country full of tarns, cushion plants, stunted snow gums and all manner of tiny alpine shrubs. There are boulders the size of huts and in the distance, pillars of rock tower into the sky. She can't wait to get there.

They haven't gone far when the temperature drops and a sudden chill wind rises. When it starts to spit, Tye and Kelly-Ann run to the shelter of the trees and put on their rain gear. It's dark in the grove and Tye breathes in the piney scent of resin, deep and refreshing. She looks at the gnarled and twisted trucks of the ancient pines.

'I could stay here forever,' she sighs.

'Me too. At least until the rain eases.'

It pelts down for ten minutes then the sun comes out again. As they leave the grove, the pools ahead glitter like jewels.

'So many!' Tye gasps.

'Land of a Thousand Lakes, they call it,' Kelly-Ann says. 'More like ten thousand.'

Soon they see a little circus of poles, coloured plastic squares, and lengths of shade cloth pegged over a sphagnum bog.

'Choose your spot while I check things out,' Kel says. 'And remember to watch where you tread. We don't want to cause more damage.'

Kelly-Ann surveys the area, moving carefully. She fixes a fallen pole here, secures a piece of shade cloth there. Squats down to examine a seedling.

Tye leaves the path and finds a place for her special tree, a sheltered nook between two rocks with a view over a tiny lake. The peaty soil is a thick mass of roots but when she digs a hole and presses her little tree into the ground it looks secure enough.

'Good luck,' she whispers.

Kel comes over and sets up the tree guard, pegging it in place.

'Future proofing,' she says. 'Aluminium poles and galvanised steel mesh.'

Tye takes a photo. It doesn't look much, just a tiny seedling in a cage in the bog, but she'll send it to Opal and Jas, and to Lukas too.

Kelly-Ann looks at the clouds. 'Typical,' she says, as it starts raining again.

They head back, lingering in the pine grove on their way. Tye suddenly worries that she may have planted her seedling too close to the rocks.

'Will it have room enough to grow?' she asks.

'It'll find its way, weather and other factors permitting.'

By the time they reach the vehicle the country behind them is covered in snow clouds.

'What's happened to the afternoon?' Kelly-Ann says. 'It'll be dark soon.'

Tye's glad they're driving slowly, not just because the night creatures are already coming out to graze but because she wants this day to last forever. The evening light begins to fade. It starts to snow. A light dusting lands on the windscreen and by the time they're nearing Chancy's it has settled on the ground.

Tye asks Kelly-Ann to drop her at the turn-off. She wants to walk.

'Thanks, Kel, thanks so much.'

'You too, Tye. You're one of our best volunteers. Can we put you down for next year?'

'For sure.'

Tye stands for a moment, watching Kelly-Ann drive away. Then she closes her eyes and holds out her hand. Snowflakes land on her palm. She thinks of her pine, nestled by its own miniature lake. Wonders how it feels, snow on its tiny branchlets for the first time. It's falling lightly here but it'll be heavier up there, maybe already deep on the ground. Is her little pencil pine happy or shocked? Happy, she decides. But so much depends on the weather. How quickly earth's temperatures rise.

There are challenges ahead, she knows, huge challenges, for her tiny tree, for herself and for the planet, but the thought of her seedling planted near the others pleases her. Tye opens her mouth and catches a snowflake on her tongue. Its cold touch makes her smile. Then she walks through the snow towards the lights of home.

Authors' Note

Lutruwita/Tasmania is renowned for its natural beauty. The Central Highlands (Big River Country) and the rugged West and Southwest contain endemic plants from ancient Gondwanan forests, also rare marsupials and endangered birds. These are increasingly under threat as our climate warms and dries and bushfires increase in intensity and frequency.

Pencil pines, *Athrotaxis cupressoides*, have grown here for at least 150 million years. They are slow-growing and may take fifty years to reach one metre in height, but individual trees can live as long as 2000 years. Unlike eucalypts they cannot regenerate after a bushfire.

Recently, dry lightning fires have become an almost annual event in Tasmania. In January 2016, after some of the driest and warmest months on record, lightning ignited eighty fires across Western Tasmania. More strikes started blazes in the Southwest in December 2018. And in January 2019 over 2000 lightning strikes sparked more than sixty bushfires. The Great Pine Tier fire in the Central Highlands was one of these.

Tyenna is about the Great Pine Tier fire. We decided to set our story near yingina – Great Lake – and tell it through the eyes of thirteen-year-old Tyenna, who is holidaying with her grandparents. Like us, Tye loves pencil pines and worries about their survival, so she's happy to take part in a pencil pine regeneration program. She is also keen to learn how First Nations people use cool burns to prevent wildfire and care for Country.

We have both lived through bushfires and know how frightening they can be. We gave Tyenna many challenges to face, including the moral dilemma of whether to disclose the presence of a runaway boy – a dilemma that becomes acute when the fire encroaches on the area where he is hiding.

Through it all, Tyenna grows into a sense of her place in the world, and an understanding of what truly matters.

Terry's bushfire experiences:
In February 1967 bushfires tore through Tasmania. I was nineteen. I remember the heat, the wind, the choking smoke of 'Black Tuesday', the sun a smeared ball in the sky, traffic lights turning blue in the eerie half-light. Sixty-four people perished that day, nine hundred were injured and hundreds of homes and public buildings were destroyed, along with livestock, native animals and tens of thousands of hectares of bush.

Later, while living in the Northern Territory, I learned from First Nations people the traditional use of fire as a tool for keeping country healthy. My fearful memories started to fade.

Then a few summers ago, a Tasmania Fire Service (TFS) worker came storming through our gate and advised us to evacuate within fifteen minutes. A nearby brush fire had got out of control. We found it hard to think coherently, to decide what to take with us. We just grabbed the laptop, our heavy boots and jackets, a few litres of water and prepared to leave. Nothing was worth risking our lives to save. We realised our fire plan was completely inadequate, that we must get serious about bushfire threat.

Julie's bushfire experience:
The 2019 fires in Tasmania were a wake-up call for me. One summer night we were having dinner outside, looking across the Huon River into the Southwest when we saw a lightshow – flashing bands of lightning moving across the hills. The next day there were fires everywhere. Weeks later I found myself standing in the same spot night after night, keeping watch. We had cars packed and ready to go. The fire glowed in the distance and black leaves were falling around me but there were no live embers, not yet. The air quality in Cygnet was as bad as Beijing and older people and parents with young kids were advised to leave because of the smoke.

It was very hot and we worked in the heat, clearing vegetation, fixing fire pumps, putting sprinklers on the roof, watching the weather, making plans and waiting, lots of waiting. Then a particularly bad day was forecast, high temperatures and strong winds. We went around the farm and said goodbye to everything we loved but the predicted weather didn't happen. The fire didn't jump the river and slowly everything returned to normal – the 'new normal' as people began calling it, a 'normal' in which climate change was suddenly real and immediate. The following summer huge mainland fires saw a pall of smoke circle the earth.

Chancy's Bay and the township of Merrick are fictional places, but the fire was real and so was the threat to land and people. That summer, the fire burned over 200 000 hectares of Tasmanian country. The impressive efforts of local people and incomers were also very real, as were the inevitable tensions and misunderstandings that occur in families during times of stress.

As co-authors, we visited the Highlands several times, speaking with community members, students, wildlife carers and local volunteer firefighters. We listened to their stories and researched the bushfire events with the assistance of scientists, TFS and emergency services personnel. We also consulted with First Nations people about cultural matters. Julie attended Indigenous fire management workshops and volunteered on a pencil pine regeneration site.

Bushfire is an all too familiar occurrence on the dry continent of Australia and its islands. In our story Tyenna faces its destructive and devastating power. She must work out her role within her family and community, as well as her responsibilities to them, to herself, to the place she loves, and to the ongoing health of the planet.

Acknowledgements

Many people generously shared their experiences of the fires with us. We are grateful to Nadine Davey and Jen Wise of Bothwell District School and to students Brodie Speed, Harley Monks, Renee Honner, Ben Branch and Robert Porter.

Many thanks to Doug Laing for his detailed account of events under the big map at Great Lake Fire Station. Thanks also to Laurence Jones for inviting us to a training night with the Bothwell Fire Brigade and to Jimmy Whittaker, Will Bowden and other members of the crew.

Thank you to the inspiring Linda McKinnell-Smith and Toni Glowacki of Great Lake Community Centre. Linda and Toni were at the heart of the action during the emergencies at Miena. Their stories helped us create our characters.

Grateful thanks to Jason Smith for sharing his knowledge of cultural burning and caring for Country.

For information on matters scientific we thank Ben French, Steve Leonard and Daniela Brozek. Thank you to wildlife carers Joy Cox and Suzy Manigian, and to Greg Irons of Bonorong Wildlife Sanctuary.

An extended interview with Dave Cleaver and Steven Richardson of Tasmania Fire Service was particularly helpful in getting an overview of the Great Pine Tier fire. Thanks also to Sandra Onn, Alison Wigston, Peter Middleton and Michael Grant of the TFS and to Ron Moss, Linton Burgess, Jenny Steigner and John Warden.

We are very grateful to our friends and colleagues, Gay McKinnon, Liz Winfield and Lian Tanner who read early drafts of the manuscript and gave excellent advice. Terry thanks her partner David for his practical support and for useful discussions.

A big thank you to Lyn White and all at Allen & Unwin for inviting us to be part of this important series, and also to Lyn and Hilary Reynolds for their invaluable work on the manuscript.

Timeline

2018 27 December
Several dry lightning strikes ignite fires at Gell River in the Franklin-Gordon Wild Rivers National Park in southwest Tasmania. Fire threatens Maydena in the Derwent Valley and Mount Field National Park.

2019 7 January
The Gell River fire continues to burn. Some New South Wales firefighters and several rotary wing aircraft are deployed. The fire burns through about 20 500 hectares and moves into peat areas.

15 January
2402 dry lightning strikes are recorded across the state, including at Miena. The strikes ignite over 70 fires as unusually dry conditions and strong winds prevail. The Great Pine Tier fire begins from a series of smaller fires, particularly at Little Pine Lagoon and Little Pine River. It burns rapidly across the Central Plateau.

16 January
Bushfire Emergency warnings are in place for Lake Fergus and Great Pine Tier as the large uncontrolled fire continues to burn. Those in the immediate area are advised to evacuate. At Mount Anne in the Southwest National Park, 50 bushwalkers are airlifted to safety.

17 January

A community meeting is held at Miena in Central Highlands as the fire takes hold at Lake Fergus. At this time of year Miena's population of 80 permanent residents is swelled by holidaymakers.

18 January

The Great Pine Tier fire spreads east to shacks at Little Pine Lagoon.

19 January

The uncontrolled bushfire threatens Miena, putting the community at 'high risk'. Residents are told to activate their bushfire survival plans immediately as winds increase fire activity and unpredictability. Local residents prepare for possible evacuation. Twelve tankers, three water bombing aircraft, five planes and eight helicopters help to hold containment lines west of Miena. The fire burns about 4500 hectares.

21 January

The Miena community continues to be under fire threat as northerly winds elevate the danger. The fire breaks containment lines and crosses the River Ouse. About 40 Miena residents are evacuated. 30 crews with aerial support fight the fire. Remote Area Teams from New Zealand are requested. Watch and Act warnings remain in place for Miena residents who choose not to leave at this point.

22 January

The Central Plateau fire near yingina – Great Lake – continues to burn in several directions. The Riveaux Road fire, near the Tahune Forest Reserve in the Huon Valley south of Hobart has now grown to 56 000 hectares.

25 January

Fire danger escalates as high temperatures and strong winds create hazardous conditions throughout the area. Firefighters spray retardant on buildings in Miena, create firebreaks and back-burn in an effort to save the town. Their efforts are rewarded. Several roads are closed in the Miena area.

27 January

An Emergency warning is issued for Miena. Residents are urged to evacuate to Bothwell Town Hall, Deloraine or Westbury. January 2019 is declared the driest month on record in Tasmania.

28 January

The road into Miena reopens to locals. Warnings remain in place and community meetings continue for Miena and surrounding areas.

3 February

187 000 hectares of Tasmania have now been exposed to fire. The Tasmania Parks and Wildlife Service fear for the survival of the endangered

pencil pines, a species endemic to Tasmania for 130 millions years.

4 February
More lightning strikes. Strong winds change to south-easterlies, threatening settlements north of Miena. Emergency warnings are listed for Reynolds Neck, Brandum, Doctors Point and Breona on the Central Plateau. The fire flares and comes within a few hundred metres of dwellings. Residents are advised to evacuate.

5 February
24 fires are still burning across the state with an estimated 195 000 hectares burnt out since fires first began in the Gell River area. The Gell River fire now covers more than 50 000 hectares with a perimeter of 692 km.

7 February
The 2019 peak fire season begins to subside when cold fronts bring widespread rain and some snow, reducing the severity of the fires. Over 40 fires have burned almost 3% of Tasmania. In the Tasmanian Wilderness World Heritage Areas, some Gondwanan vegetation is damaged but does not experience the devastation caused by the 2016 fires.

Although many small communities have had to evacuate, there has been no loss of life. Hobart and several Huon Valley communities suffer acute air pollution during the fires.

Just over 200 000 hectares were burnt in the 2018–2019 fire season, the most extensive area since the 1967 fires. The lightning storms responsible for most of the fires continue to increase in occurrence due to climate change.

21 February

The Tasmania Parks and Wildlife Service and Tasmania Fire Service continue to extinguish hot spots in areas affected by the Great Pine Tier fire on the Central Plateau.

Find out more about...

2018–2019 Tasmanian Bushfires
https://knowledge.aidr.org.au/resources/2018-19-bushfire-tas-tasmanian-bushfires/
https://wildfiretoday.com/tag/gell-river-fire/
https://www.youtube.com
Search for '94,000 hectares of forest burnt in Tasmania's summer of fire 2019'

The Great Pine Tier Fire and Miena
https://www.examiner.com.au/story/5861230/miena-evacuated-as-fire-breaks-containment-lines/
https://www.abc.net.au
Search for 'Tasmanian small town of Miena ready to flee as bushfire sends smoke skywards'
https://aidr.org.au
Search for 'Tasmanian bushfires, 2018–2019'

First Nations Burning Practices
https://www.youtube.com
Search for 'Should Tasmania go back to traditional burning practices? ABC Australia'
Search for 'Fire Country: The revival of cultural burning practices | Victor Steffensen'

Pencil Pines and Climate Change
https://www.youtube.com
Search for 'Tasmania on fire: Is this what climate change looks like?'

General Bushfire Texts

Cummings, Phil, illustrated by Andrew McLean. *Through the Smoke*, Scholastic Australia, 2019

Lesley, John. *Bushfires in Australia*, Redback Publishing, 2020

Murphy, Sally. *My Australian Story: Bushfire*, Scholastic Australia, 2019

Steffensen, Victor. *Fire Country: How Indigenous Fire Management Could Help Save Australia*, Hardie Grant Explore, 2020

THROUGH MY EYES

COMING SOON

A powerful story of one girl's experience of 2019's Cyclone Veronica in Western Australia

THROUGH MY EYES — NATURAL DISASTER ZONES

A powerful and moving fiction series about children living in contemporary natural disaster zones.

www.throughmyeyesbooks.com.au